Science and Engineering Projects Using the Arduino and Raspberry Pi

Explore STEM Concepts with Microcomputers

Paul Bradt
David Bradt

Apress®

Science and Engineering Projects Using the Arduino and Raspberry Pi:
Explore STEM Concepts with Microcomputers

Paul Bradt
Houston, TX, USA

David Bradt
Houston, USA

ISBN-13 (pbk): 978-1-4842-5810-1
https://doi.org/10.1007/978-1-4842-5811-8

ISBN-13 (electronic): 978-1-4842-5811-8

Managing Director, Apress Media LLC: Welmoed Spahr
Acquisitions Editor: Aaron Black
Development Editor: James Markham
Coordinating Editor: Jessica Vakili

Distributed to the book trade worldwide by Springer Science+Business Media New York, 233 Spring Street, 6th Floor, New York, NY 10013. Phone 1-800-SPRINGER, fax (201) 348-4505, e-mail orders-ny@springer-sbm.com, or visit www.springeronline.com. Apress Media, LLC is a California LLC and the sole member (owner) is Springer Science + Business Media Finance Inc (SSBM Finance Inc). SSBM Finance Inc is a **Delaware** corporation.

For information on translations, please e-mail rights@apress.com, or visit http://www.apress.com/rights-permissions.

Apress titles may be purchased in bulk for academic, corporate, or promotional use. eBook versions and licenses are also available for most titles. For more information, reference our Print and eBook Bulk Sales web page at http://www.apress.com/bulk-sales.

Any source code or other supplementary material referenced by the author in this book is available to readers on GitHub via the book's product page, located at www.apress.com/978-1-4842-5810-1. For more detailed information, please visit http://www.apress.com/source-code.

Printed on acid-free paper

*The authors dedicate this book to
all of the Science, Technology, Engineering,
Math (STEM) teachers who guide and
shape the paths of many young minds (including ours)
to question, learn, and utilize new technology to
solve problems. Without these unsung heroes,
the world would not have powerful cell phones,
highly reliable cars, the Internet, and many other
amazing things we routinely take for granted.*

Table of Contents

TABLE OF CONTENTS

About the Authors

Paul Bradt has a BS in Computer Science from the University of Houston–Clear Lake. He currently owns a small business and writes books, develops code, and does IT support work. He has experimented with the Arduino and Raspberry Pi system and believes them to be excellent tools for developing an understanding of electronic components and hardware interaction in integrated systems. He believes they are very useful as a teaching aid in learning computer programming, science, and engineering. He likes to perform sophisticated troubleshooting of computer problems and has found that online resources can be a great help for novice users to get their experiments operating quickly and effectively.

David Bradt has a BS in Mechanical Engineering from New Mexico State University with many years of experience in the aerospace industry and in the petrochemical industry. He enjoys building and designing devices to measure and control systems. He has found the Arduino and Raspberry Pi to be incredibly powerful little devices that with a little bit of work can do many different tasks. He is a big fan of *Star Trek: The Original Series* and astronomy.

About the Technical Reviewer

Sri Manikanta Palakollu is an undergraduate student pursuing his bachelor's degree in Computer Science and Engineering at SICET under JNTUH. He is a founder of the OpenStack Developer Community in his college. He started his journey as a competitive programmer. He always loves to solve problems that are related to the data science field. His interests include data science, app development, web development, cybersecurity, and technical writing. He has published many articles on data science, machine learning, programming, and cybersecurity in publications like Hacker Noon, freeCodeCamp, Noteworthy, and DDI through the Medium platform.

Acknowledgments

This book would not be possible without the authors' gaining early technical insight regarding the Raspberry Pi and Arduino from others. Jared Brank and Dennis Pate provided a lot of basic information, key insights, and Arduino hardware early in the process. The authors thank the following individuals who listened to them on many occasions and provided help, insight, and inspiration with their own experiences with the Raspberry Pi and other projects: Jeff Dunehew, Todd Franke, and Fitz Walker. Additionally, significant assistance with 3D printing was provided by Mitch Long and David Thoerig.

Producing this book would not have been possible without the excellent help and guidance regarding scope and early editorial reviews by Joanna Opaskar and Ed Weisblatt. The authors also utilized many ideas from Andrew Bradt and Laura Brank's science fair experience. Most important was the support and advice from Andrea Bradt.

Introduction

The authors' journey developing this book started in 2013 when they discovered the Arduino microcontroller. It is interesting how something big really starts with one step as they found the Arduino incredibly powerful. Users are able to program it with computer code, and then it executes its instructions for as long as it has power. The authors started evaluating various applications of the Arduino around the house and in their hobby endeavors. In 2017, they started experimenting with the Raspberry Pi minicomputer which enables users to take projects to a whole new level with a low-cost computer that interfaces with sensors. Since a Raspberry Pi is very affordable, a real computer can now be dedicated to operating a system permanently. While requiring some technical steps to set up, both of these tools can be used to gather data, automate tasks, and provide a lot of fun. The authors found it very satisfying to watch a device do several tasks, especially when they set it up. This book chronicles some science and engineering projects the authors developed over the past few years and provides helpful hints, along with a few things to avoid.

There are two primary areas of focus or goals of this book. The first goal is to help the reader explore the Arduino and Raspberry Pi. The second goal is exploring science and engineering in interesting and fun ways.

The projects and concepts in this book are meant to accomplish the first goal by providing information to get an Arduino or Raspberry Pi system set up, running, and ready to capture data. The text provides enough detail for users with average assembly or electrical skills to complete them. Additionally, the goals of learning are to gain knowledge and skills. When the reader engages in a project that requires them to try new things, it reinforces how they learn and gain confidence and encourages them to try even more complex tools and techniques.

The second goal is exploring concepts of STEM (**S**cience, **T**echnology, **E**ngineering, **M**athematics) and working through examples to demonstrate basic scientific and engineering concepts. Finally, the authors provide some detail on the mathematics needed to understand and explain the science demonstrated.

Science and engineering provide critical skill sets for the modern world that can be used in everyday life. People use these skills to develop the technology that the modern world relies on. This book can establish these skill sets for a fruitful and rewarding career.

The authors hope this book inspires the reader to expand and explore their own STEM projects by including a wide range from beginner to advanced. From these examples, the reader can learn many techniques, tools, and technologies and apply them beyond the ones listed here; but first, the authors introduce STEM.

What Is STEM?

STEM (**S**cience, **T**echnology, **E**ngineering, **M**athematics) is a program based on educating students in science, technology, engineering, and mathematics in an integrated, interdisciplinary approach to learning.

School systems today strive to improve education in STEM. This goal is an area where educators can use outside help developing and improving students' knowledge when they actively contribute, design, and build hands-on projects. In many ways, the young mind is excited and motivated building projects. They develop an in-depth understanding of what is required and how it works. The authors believe this is the best way to learn and remember these concepts, which results in a solid STEM foundation for students.

A question not often understood is how the scientific method is different from an engineering approach. Understanding the difference between science and engineering can be seen in the original *Star Trek* series.

Mr. Spock was the science officer, and Montgomery Scott (Scotty) was the chief engineer. Their jobs and how they approached new scenarios or problems really provide a great explanation about the differences and similarities between science and engineering. Let's examine some examples.

Mr. Spock used the term fascinating when describing a new event or phenomenon. The role of science is to expand knowledge and investigate new events. This fascination with new and unique areas is key for a scientist. Scotty, the engineer, on the other hand always had to fix the warp engines, the transporter, or some other critical system. The normal role of an engineer is to develop and implement solutions to problems. In one of the episodes, Scotty indicated he would rather read his engineering journals to learn about how others solved problems than go on shore leave!

Science

Researchers use the scientific method as a tool to understand questions in their area of interest. Based on the information they have initially, they develop a hypothesis and then methods to test the validity of the hypothesis. When sufficient test data are gathered and analyzed, the researcher either accepts or rejects the hypothesis. In many cases, positive or negative results point to the next step or direction of exploration and contribute to the general body of scientific and engineering knowledge.

Engineering

The primary goal of engineering is to evaluate alternatives and choose the optimal solution to minimize or eliminate specific problems or issues. Solutions are not necessarily new, but may be repurposed concepts applied to different problem areas. Other aspects of engineering include planning the work, selecting components to meet requirements, and following through on managing and completing a project. Often projects or systems fail because the planning, scheduling, and logistics of activities are not adequately engineered for an optimum solution. These skills are important and necessary in any job.

Science and engineering use many of the same tools and techniques, but it is important to understand the distinction between scientific experimentation and the engineering process of developing optimal solutions. For one thing, they both use the language of mathematics to describe percentages, results, probability, and other physical parameters. However, science's goal is to expand knowledge which is different than engineering's goal of selecting an optimum solution and proceeding with solving the problem. One other difference is a scientific test often gains new knowledge, whereas an engineering test often demonstrates how a system performs a function. In many ways, they are synergistic as science often provides new tools and ideas for engineers to use to solve problems.

In the authors' minds, the roots of some key technological advancements that exist now can be traced back 50 years to the original *Star Trek* TV show. For example, in the show, they used tricorders to gather data about aliens, equipment failures, medical problems, and a host of other out of this world challenges. They had communicators that allowed them to contact crewmembers all over alien worlds. Finally, they had the replicators that allowed them to produce any type of food they desired. Today we don't have tricorders, but we do have some examples that 50 years ago would have been amazing. Today there are personal computers, cell phones, 3D printing, and incredible sensors based on the early transistors of the 1960s. The Arduino and the Raspberry Pi, two examples of new technology, can be built into devices similar to the incredibly versatile *Star Trek* tricorders.

Both Mr. Spock and Scotty realized they needed each other (science and engineering) to accomplish the goals of exploration and keep the Enterprise flying safely through space. In today's complex world, integrating science and engineering is key to researching problems and developing solutions.

In the following chapters, the authors will demonstrate all of the components of STEM needed to research scientific questions, use new technology (Arduino and Raspberry Pi), employ engineering techniques, and use mathematics to quantify the scientific data. As *Star Trek* boldly went forth to explore new worlds, the authors hope the students of today do the same!

CHAPTER 1

Key Technology Tools

This chapter will highlight some of the basics about the Arduino and the Raspberry Pi. It will help the reader get started if they are unfamiliar with these powerful devices. It is amazing what these devices can do and this chapter provides some basic aspects for getting them set up to run.

Arduino Basics

The Arduino is a powerful microcontroller that is ready to program and acts as an intermediary device between a personal computer and various sensors. It is relatively new technology that is a great tool for gaining insight into physical properties and other scientific parameters.

The Arduino board was first developed in Italy in 2004 as a tool to help train students in programming. It is an open source tool and as such has developed a large base of helpful web sites and user groups. It represents a breakthrough as an easy-to-use, relatively inexpensive, programmable interface between a computer and various sensors. The software development package and all of the online resources help make this an ideal data logging tool for science fair/college projects.

The Arduino, Adafruit, SparkFun, Hacktronics, and other web sites are great places to start. There are also several introductory books to help the researcher get started using this device. *Getting started with Arduino* by Banzi is a very good beginner's book on Arduino.

Other sources of information for the Arduino novice are maker faires and user group activities.

© Paul Bradt and David Bradt 2020
P. Bradt and D. Bradt, *Science and Engineering Projects Using the Arduino and Raspberry Pi*,
https://doi.org/10.1007/978-1-4842-5811-8_1

1

There are several versions and sizes, but for the projects in this book, the Arduino Uno and the Integrated Development Environment (IDE) version 1.89 were utilized. Figure 1-1 shows an example of the Arduino Uno. The authors recommend for the person unfamiliar with Arduinos to use an official version and not a clone. The authors have never experienced a problem with an official Arduino, but there are many clones, and the authors have experienced problems with one of them.

Figure 1-1. *Arduino Uno*

Arduino Setup

Setting up an Arduino is relatively straightforward; the reader should follow these basic steps to get the device running:

1. The Arduino is connected to a computer via a USB connection to the input port (see Figure 1-3).

2. Load code using the IDE (see Figure 1-2).

3. Open the serial monitor to get data.

These steps sound basic, and after the reader completes these steps a few times, they will see how easy it is to connect and run an Arduino. In many cases, the challenges occur with the code. If the reader is copying code from a source, it is important to type it in exactly as it looks. Even then there could be errors, but that is part of the adventure, and it's very rewarding when the code runs.

Figure 1-2. *Arduino IDE*

Ports and Interfaces

Figure 1-3 shows the main ports of the Arduino Uno.

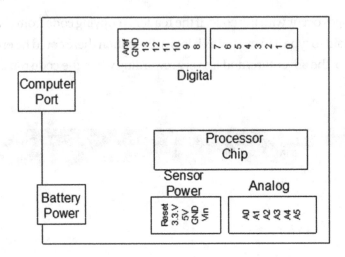

Figure 1-3. *Arduino Ports*

There are five primary port groupings that are used to connect to the Arduino:

Computer port: This is the primary port that is directly connected to the computer. It is a micro-USB port that powers and enables the user to upload the sketches or programs to the Arduino.

Battery power port: This port allows an Arduino to be unplugged from a computer and use battery power to operate. A standard wall power supply that provides 9–12 V DC can also be used.

Sensor power ports: These plug connections provide 3.3 V and 5 V DC power. There is also a reset connection and input voltage connection.

Analog device ports: These connections are for analog inputs.

Digital device ports: These are for digital inputs and outputs.

IDE (Integrated Development Environment):
The IDE is the program that is used to develop the code. It is the programming tool that runs on a computer and has features to help the developer write code. The IDE tool must be downloaded from the Arduino web site.

Sketch: The code that runs on an Arduino is called a sketch. Once the code is developed in the IDE, it is uploaded to the Arduino.

Libraries: These are code modules that are installed on the Arduino and called up by the program when needed. Libraries add a lot of functionality and do not require any additional coding.

There are other components and hardware that can be used with the Arduino:

Shields/breakout boards: These are add-on boards that are either inserted into the standard Arduino board ports or connected via wires.

Sensors: A sensor is a device that senses some type of data. It can be used to directly measure a physical aspect, or it can be used with some mathematics to infer a physical measurement.

Effectors: An effector imparts some change in the physical world when activated. Motors, solenoids, and servos are some examples.

LCDs: Liquid Crystal Display can be used to show data.

LEDs: Light-Emitting Diodes or other incandescent lights can also indicate an event has occurred.

Lessons Learned About the Arduino

The Arduino is relatively easy to use, but the authors found there are a few key points that will help when using this powerful device:

- Each Arduino attaches to a specific com port. The port may have to be changed or selected in the tools tab under "port" to get the IDE to recognize the Arduino.

- If the code is being pasted into the IDE, do not copy from Microsoft Word or another word processor. First, put it in a text editor such as Notepad, Notepad++, or some other C/C++ IDE editor and then copy it from there. Important note: Notepad and Notepad++ are not development tools like the IDE. One other very important item of note is when the code was transcribed into the book format some of the code text that must be on one line may show up on two lines in this book. The authors have tried their best to highlight the code that should be on one line in the IDE by bolding it in the Listing. Please contact the authors if there are questions at contact@pdanalytic.com.

- It is a good idea to test the devices with a basic program to be sure they work, before moving to a more complex program.

- If the final code is complex, get each piece of code working before adding more modules. This way, it is easier to find the module where the problem is located.

- The authors recommend for long timing events or complex programs to not use the "delay command," because it locks the Arduino and prevents it from doing anything else. Instead, use the "milli command" that tracks time intervals between events and still allows other actions to occur. The milli code might be a little more complex, but it allows the Arduino to perform other functions simultaneously. Using the delay command for short events or simple programs like the ones in this book, such as a switch debounce, is recommended.

- A feature built into the Arduino IDE is the "auto-format command." It can be found under the tools tab or using "Alt+T." This command helps identify missing items and also helps organize the code for improved readability.

- One more key aspect of Arduino coding is the "loop command." There are a few different types, but common ones such as "void loop" and the "for command" perform several operations and then repeat them.

- Check the wiring twice before applying power. It can be difficult to see which port a wire is plugged into when there are several wires.

- It is hard to know what code is on an Arduino. One easy way that helps determine what is loaded on an Arduino is saving code with a descriptive name, date, and even time information. This helps programmers who may need to go back to a previous code version.

- One other very helpful trick is to put the descriptive name of the code on a piece of tape and stick it on top of the computer port. This helps when working on, or programing, several different Arduinos.

- One of the advantages of the Arduino is that once it is programmed, it remembers the code. When a power source is plugged into the battery power port, it will operate the Arduino. According to the Arduino web site, any power source that can supply 9–12 V DC, 250 mA, or more will work. The plug must be 2.1 mm with the center pin providing positive voltage and the exterior of the plug the negative terminal. Some power supplies do not deliver enough current or do not provide stable power. If an Arduino is behaving strangely, try a different power supply.

- Some programs need special ways to use and communicate with the Arduino. To do this, the reader should understand these special connection ports on the Arduino Uno: analog A5 is the SCL (Clock port) and A4 is the SDA (Data port).

Raspberry Pi Basics

The Raspberry Pi 3 is a powerful minicomputer. This piece of technology comes with a lot of features like any other modern computer. It is an experimental/hobbyist device developed around 2011 in the United Kingdom to teach programming. For its low cost, it has many capabilities and allows the user to configure it in many ways. There are several models on the market. For this book, the authors choose the Raspberry Pi 3 Model B V1.2 (Figures 1-4 and 1-5). There is a new Raspberry Pi 4 that was recently released that has more features. The authors researched the setup and use of the Raspberry Pi 4, and it appears to be the same as the Raspberry Pi 3. We believe these projects will work the same if you have a Raspberry Pi 4.

Figure 1-4. *Raspberry Pi*

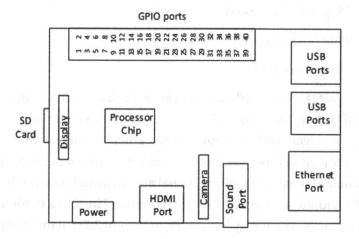

Figure 1-5. *Raspberry Pi Ports*

Once the Raspberry Pi 3 is up and running, it is just like a normal personal computer. It has a graphical user interface (GUI) similar to any computer that enables you to open programs or files with the click of a mouse. It uses a version of the Linux program for the operating system (OS) called Debian, so it is a bit of a hobbyist machine and occasionally may have an issue. There are a lot of online resources to find help.

9

The Raspberry Pi 3 has a 1.2 GHz 64-bit quad-core CPU, 1 GB RAM, an integrated wireless connection, four USB ports, an Ethernet port, and an HDMI connection. It is a truly powerful device for only ≈ $25. The Raspberry Pi 4 has a 1.4 GHz 64-bit quad core CPU, options of 2, 4, 8 GB RAM and costs from $35 to 75. The Raspberry Pi 4 will run hotter than the Pi 3 and it is recommended to have a cooling fan but it is faster.

Raspberry Pi Setup

These are the general steps to set up the Pi:

1. Insert the SD card.

2. Plug in the monitor.

3. Plug in the keyboard.

4. Plug in the mouse.

5. Start the system.

The authors recommend that the reader do all their programming in versions of Python 3.X or later. The exception to this recommendation is if the reader has legacy code that runs on an earlier version like Python 2.7.X.

Some projects in this book require additional modules to run. The "pip" command is typed into the terminal area to install code modules. The reader should be aware that the pip command installs a module in the base Python area, which may be specific to Python 2.7.3. If the reader has upgraded to or is using a newer version of Python, they will need to use pip3 or Python 3.

Operating the Raspberry Pi is much like a personal computer. It has a GUI along with several programs such as a spreadsheet, word processor, and other built-in items. Figure 1-6 provides an example of the interface.

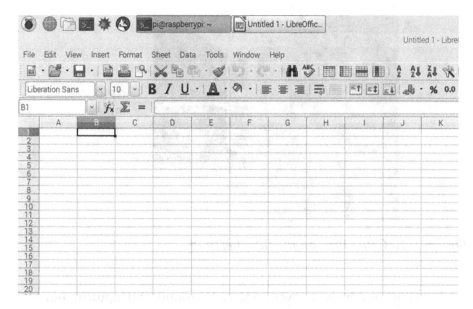

Figure 1-6. Raspberry Pi GUI with Spreadsheet

For the purposes of this book, the authors will focus primarily on how to connect sensors to the Raspberry Pi and get data out of them. There are many other uses for the Raspberry Pi that will not be covered in this text.

Figure 1-7 shows the General-Purpose Input/Output or GPIO pins, although it may not be easy to determine the pin number on the Raspberry Pi. A ribbon cable is also shown that connects to a nice interface board made by MCM. This interface board has pin numbers and makes it a lot easier to connect sensors to the Raspberry Pi. More about this in the next chapter.

Figure 1-7. *GPIO Pins on the Raspberry Pi*

The GPIO pins include several 5 V, 3.3 V, ground, and input/output ports.

There are several special ports on the GPIO pins. These are very important for the Raspberry Pi to communicate via Serial Peripheral Interface (SPI) protocol with other devices like an analog to digital converter (ADC). For the Raspberry Pi 3, pin 23 is the GPIO SPI clock connection; this is also called GPIO11. The next two special connections are pin numbers 19 and 21. Pin 19 is the data in connection termed Master Out Slave In (MOSI), also called GPIO10. Pin 21 is the data out connection termed Master In Slave Out (MISO), also called GPIO9. The final connection is pin 24 and it is the chip enable (CE0) connection. There are a lot of confusing descriptions and diagrams on the Internet regarding these connections, but once the authors understood what these four connections were used for, it started making sense.

Many resources are available online, and the following books were helpful in explaining the Raspberry Pi and its features. *Beginner's Guide to Raspberry Pi* published by BDM Publications, *Raspberry Pi: The Complete Manual* published by Image Publishing, *Learn Raspberry Pi Programming with Python* published by Apress, and *The Python Coding Manual* published by BDM Publications are good resources.

The following are some Raspberry Pi terms and definitions:

GUI: Graphical user interface, a user interface that allows interaction with computers or other electronic devices through graphical icons or visual pointers.

HDMI: High-definition multimedia interface is the standard connection for high-definition (HD) and ultra-high-definition (UHD) equipment.

Debian Linux: Operating system that is similar to Linux and is composed entirely of free software. The group which maintains it is called Debian.

Python: A programming language for general-purpose programming that was created in 1991 by Guido van Rossum.

Raspberry Pi IDE: Some of the graphics in this book may show the Python 3.5.9 interface; others show the Thonny interface which has Python 3.7 embedded in it.

Tkinter: This program or module is included in Python and is a great tool to develop GUIs for the Raspberry Pi.

sudo raspi-config: Command typed into the terminal that opens the rasp-config tool. In this tool, the user can select the one wire, Inter-Integrated Circuit (I2C), or SPI protocols for connecting with remote devices (Figure 1-8).

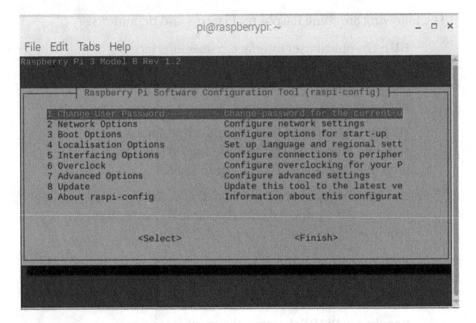

Figure 1-8. *Raspi-config*

Terminal: Program where commands are typed in
to execute on the Raspberry Pi (Figure 1-9).

Picamera: Refers to a Raspberry camera computer code
module.

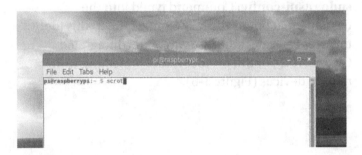

Figure 1-9. *Terminal Interface*

Lessons Learned About the Raspberry Pi

The authors learned several items as they worked on these projects with the Raspberry Pi. The following items may help the reader set up their own systems:

- Keyboard configuration: The reader may find when they first start out and type a command in on the keyboard that the wrong character may show up on the screen. In the authors' case, the Raspberry Pi 3 was configured for a keyboard in a different country. To fix this, the reader should visit the Stack Exchange site as most likely the keyboard is set for a UK version. US or other countries' keyboards have a slightly different mapping arrangement.

  This site has more info on this change: `https://raspberrypi.stackexchange.com/questions/236/simple-keyboard-configuration`.

- An important lesson the authors learned is that the Raspberry Pi 3 power supply needs to deliver the correct amount of current required. The authors needed two power supplies: one for the touchscreen and one for the Raspberry Pi. The touchscreen power supply did not put out enough current for the Raspberry Pi and caused it to crash often.

- Timing issue: You may notice that if you want precision control of timing, the Raspberry Pi program may be off by a few milliseconds. This is partially due to Raspberry Pi not being a real-time system and partially due to Raspberry Pi's Linux-derived operating system (OS) overhead. You can find many examples of real-time systems in the real world. One example of a real-time system is how a microwave, when the door is opened, immediately shuts off so that the person operating it is not exposed to harmful microwaves. Real-time systems have to be able to react rapidly to interrupts. This is different from a personal computer, generally known as general-purpose system, an OS where interrupts don't take priority due to how the chipset is designed. General-purpose systems provide multiple functions which take some minimum amount of time to execute. All general-purpose OSs have some form of overhead that comes in various forms from longer boot-up time to latency between receiving an interrupt event for a new unscheduled task. The Arduino operates closer to real time, so if the reader needs to know the time data is taken, then they might want to consider using the Arduino instead of the Raspberry Pi.

- One other key difference between the Raspberry Pi and the Arduino is the voltage needed to power them. The Raspberry Pi uses 5 V DC. The Arduino can use 9–12 V DC. It is critical not to use a power supply meant for an Arduino on a Raspberry Pi; it will damage it.

- Unlike the Arduino, the Raspberry Pi does not have a built-in analog to digital converter. Therefore, when using analog sensors, the reader may need to place an analog to digital converter between the sensor and the Raspberry Pi.

- The Raspberry Pi will need to be configured for either an I2C device or Serial Peripheral Interface (SPI). The following steps can configure the Raspberry Pi for I2C or SPI:

  - Run sudo raspi-config in the terminal window.

  - Use the down arrow to select 5, Interfacing Options.

- Arrow down to P4 SPI or P5 I2C.

- Select yes to enable the correct protocol.

- Many Raspberry PI programs use modules. Some of these modules are included in the Python code like Tkinter. This is used in the astrophotography project. Other modules are not included, in particular, Adafruit_GPIO.SPI and Adafruit_MCP3008, which are used in several projects in this book.

- When installing modules like Adafruit_GPIO. SPI and Adafruit_MCP3008, the user must ensure they are installed in the correct folder. Use pip3 or pip2 depending on the version of Python on the Raspberry Pi.

- The Raspberry Pi may come with an SD card with the operating system. However, the reader may download the operating system and install it on an SD card. When formatting an SD card for the Raspberry Pi operating system, run the Guiformat program to create an exFAT (also known as 32-bit FAT) SD card and leave all options at default. This web site has some helpful info: `www.raspberrypi.org/documentation/ installation/sdxc_formatting.md`.

- Finally, the authors used two different programming tools on the Raspberry Pi. They are Python3 and Thonny. They seem to behave very similar and have very similar graphical user interfaces.

Basic Electronics Definitions

The projects in this book include some basic electronic methods and devices. The following definitions may be useful if the reader is new to electronics:

Current: Flow of electrons in a circuit. Units are in amps or milliamps.

Integrated circuit: The integrated circuit ushered in the modern era of electronics. The concept is adding components to a single device which decreases size, increases speed, and lowers the cost of manufacturing. The Arduino and Raspberry Pi have several integrated circuit chips on them.

Resistor: Device that resists the flow of electrons in a circuit. Units are in ohms. The symbol is an omega (Ω). The force sensor used in this book is a variable resistance device that as the force is increased, the resistance decreases.

Transistor: This component is key to most modern electronics. Several of the temperature-measuring devices used in this book are a transistor. They normally have three connections: power, ground, and signal. As the temperature changes, the signal output changes proportionally.

Voltage: In order for current to flow through a circuit, there needs to be difference of energy. The measure for this is voltage, and the normal symbol is V.

Summary

This chapter provides some basic information about two very powerful technology tools: the Arduino and the Raspberry Pi. The reader may want to refer back to the "Lessons Learned" sections if they run into any problems using the devices. Additionally, there is a lot of information online and answers to specific questions, along with user groups and maker spaces that can provide the novice Arduino and Raspberry Pi user answers to their questions.

CHAPTER 2

Data Logging Basics

In *Star Trek,* the characters used tricorders to capture data. The technology we have today is not as advanced as that in *Star Trek,* but still very amazing. The next step in this book is to start using this technology to obtain scientific information. This chapter covers information that is very important for someone just starting with either the Arduino or Raspberry Pi and provides a few easy methods to save data using them. This is called data logging and is useful to save the information to be utilized at a later date. The STEM principles in this chapter include

---

Science   Measuring temperature of the environment.

Technology/Engineering   Using the Arduino, Raspberry Pi, and two types of temperature sensors. Gain an understanding on the difference between analog and digital sensors.

Mathematics   Programming temperature conversions and graphing the data.

While the reader may want to skip this chapter and go on to other more advanced projects, it is recommended to look over these projects and try them if the reader is unfamiliar with the Arduino or Raspberry Pi.

© Paul Bradt and David Bradt 2020
P. Bradt and D. Bradt, *Science and Engineering Projects Using the Arduino and Raspberry Pi,*
https://doi.org/10.1007/978-1-4842-5811-8_2

Data Logging with the Arduino

The easiest method shown in this book to log and capture data is to set up an Arduino to send data to the computer. Then use the IDE serial monitor to observe and save the data. Once the correct data is obtained, it is easy to copy using "Ctrl+C" after it is highlighted and then paste it into a spreadsheet or another document.

The parts needed are relatively straightforward to use the Arduino Uno and the serial monitor to gather data from a simple temperature sensor. The sensor used in this project is the MCP9700. It is a relatively inexpensive device and in this case is configured just like a standard transistor. This device is an analog sensor, which means the output is directly related to temperature and it can vary infinitely over the range. There is a flat side, and the leads must be connected as shown in Figures 2-1 and 2-2.

The parts needed are

- Arduino Uno

- MCP9700 temp sensor (output is 10 mV per °C with a 500 mV offset)

- Miscellaneous wires to connect to the sensor

Figure 2-1. *Arduino and Basic Temperature Sensor*

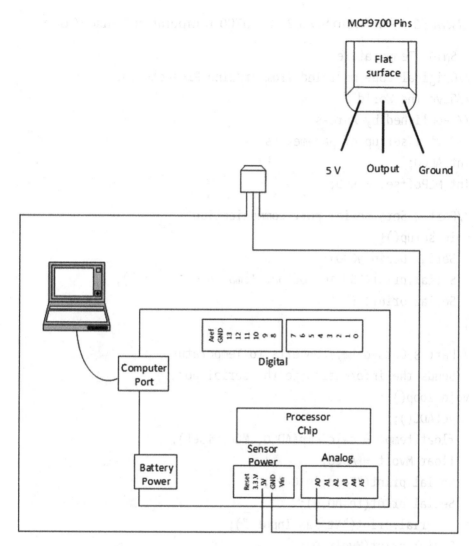

Figure 2-2. *Arduino and Temperature Sensor Schematic*

Listing 2-1 provides the basic code that the user will need to upload via the IDE. This code outputs the data in degree Celsius along with the raw data from the sensor.

Listing 2-1. Arduino SN102 MCP9700 Temperature Sensor Code

```
//SN102_Temperature
//Original code modified from Arduino Projects to
//Save the World
// Published by Apress
//Part 1 set up of parameters
int ADC0;
int MCPoffset = 500;

//Part 2 Sets serial port communication
void setup(){
  Serial.begin(9600);
  Serial.print("SN 102 Output Temp in C 5 sec: ");
  Serial.println(" ");
}

//Part 3 Gets data, converts to Temperature
//Sends the information to the serial port
void loop() {
  getADC();
  float temp0 = calcTemp(ADC0, MCPoffset);
  float Mvolt = ADC0;
  Serial.print("Temp in C ");
  Serial.print(temp0,0);
    Serial.print("\t Raw Input ");
  Serial.print(Mvolt,0);
  Serial.println(" ");
  delay(5000);
}
void getADC() {
  ADC0 = analogRead(A0);
```

```
}
float calcTemp (int val,int offset) {
  return((val*4.8828)-offset)/10;
}
```

The preceding code has three main parts. They are labeled as Parts 1, 2, and 3. The first part sets up parameter which is MCPoffest for this type of temperature sensor. The second part starts up the serial port. The third part of this code starts the loop that gets the data from the sensor, converts the data from the sensor to Celsius temperature, and then posts it to the serial monitor.

The best way for the reader to learn the symbols and the code language is to try several simple pieces of code, Blink being one which is located in the Arduino examples folder in basics. This simple code does not require any wiring; it blinks an LED that is located on the Arduino. Gaining experience and looking at these simple pieces of code gets the reader on the path of acquiring the ability to read code.

Also note in the preceding code the symbol // is used to comment out a line so it does not run. This is helpful to explain the code and document aspects.

Once the Arduino is running, it is easy to access the data from its serial USB connection to the computer. Simply click the Serial Monitor button on the Arduino IDE tool as seen in Figure 2-3.

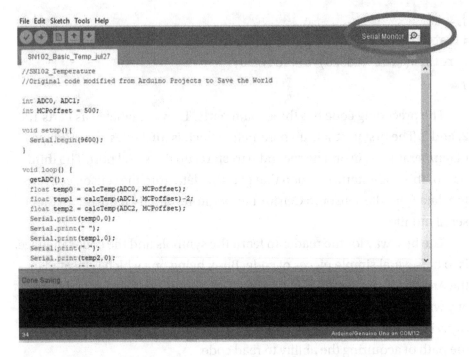

Figure 2-3. Serial Monitor in the Arduino IDE

An example of serial data from Arduino is shown in Figure 2-4. Note it is highlighted which allows it to be copied using "Ctrl+C" and then pasted into another file using "Ctrl+V." The investigator may need to unplug the Arduino and stop the data coming across the serial port to capture it as it will continue to update as long as the Arduino has power. Figure 2-4 exemplifies the type of data and information sent over the serial port to the computer using Arduino as the bridge. The investigator can tailor the information inside the Arduino program so that the important data can be selected, formatted, and sent over the serial line to the computer.

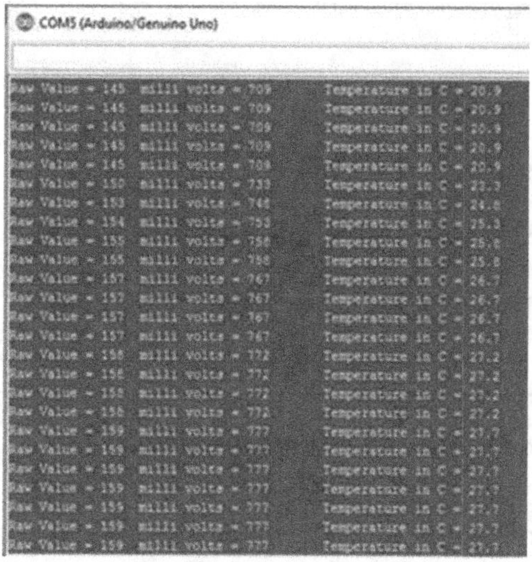

Figure 2-4. *Highlighted Data in the Serial Monitor*

A new feature in the Arduino IDE serial monitor is the ability to have it apply a time stamp each time data is taken. This does not require any code and makes it very easy to capture this information.

After copying the data and inserting it into a spreadsheet, the user needs to select how to limit (increment) the data. This means how the data is separated so the spreadsheet determines how to place it in individual cells.

Once copied and pasted into a spreadsheet, it can be displayed as a graph. Figure 2-5 shows what a common graph looks like in Excel or any other spreadsheet program.

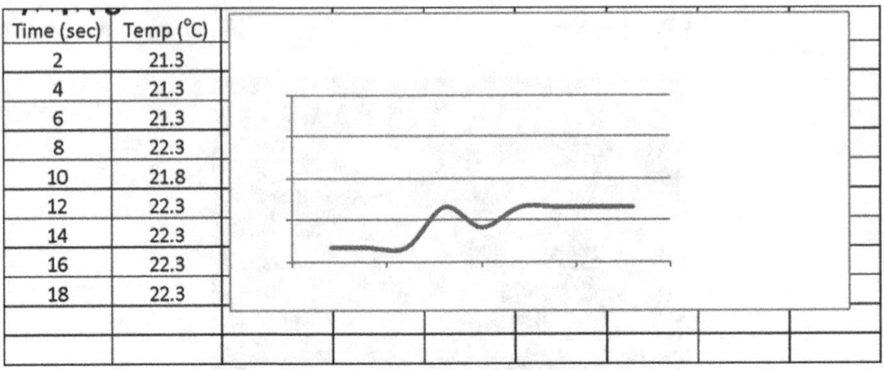

Time (sec)	Temp (°C)
2	21.3
4	21.3
6	21.3
8	22.3
10	21.8
12	22.3
14	22.3
16	22.3
18	22.3

Figure 2-5. *Excel Graph of Temperature Data*

Another method of data logging will be discussed in a later chapter using a data logging shield. This board allows the user to set up the Arduino so it will collect data and save it in a file on an SD card on the shield without being connected to the computer. The SD card can be removed later from the Arduino shield to download the data to the computer.

Data Logging with the Raspberry Pi

The Raspberry Pi is a very low-cost technological breakthrough in a real personal computer that provides a lot of options for capturing and managing data. In this example, the authors will demonstrate how to capture and log data in a very similar way as was used on the Arduino in the previous section. One advantage of the Raspberry Pi is it has a built-in spreadsheet so that the data can stay on the device.

This project uses a different temperature sensor that is a bit more complex.

The parts needed are

- Raspberry Pi 3

- MCM 40-pin GPIO breakout board and cable for Raspberry Pi (or equivalent)

- DS18B20 waterproof temperature sensor (one-wire temperature sensor)

- 4.7K ohm resistor

- Miscellaneous wires, proto-board, and terminal strips

The company MCM makes a 40-pin GPIO breakout board that has the power channels set up nicely for use (Figure 2-6 shows the 5 V connection on the left and 3.3 V connection on the right). There are other GPIO breakout boards available that are similar, but this one has the 5 V and 3.3 V connections directly to the proto-board which is helpful.

This project uses a digital sensor. It has additional circuitry inside the device and outputs a digital value given the temperature. It increments in whole steps over the range. Since it is digital, the Raspberry Pi can readily accept the digital signal. The setup of the Raspberry Pi and the MCM breakout board connected to the temperature sensor is shown in Figure 2-6.

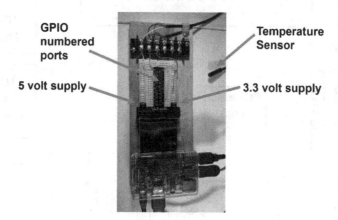

Figure 2-6. *Raspberry Pi Connected to DS18B20 Temperature Sensor*

Figure 2-7 shows the numbering of the IO ports. The 3.3 V and ground can be connected to any of the ports that provide those items. Port 1 is 3.3 V and port 6 is a ground.

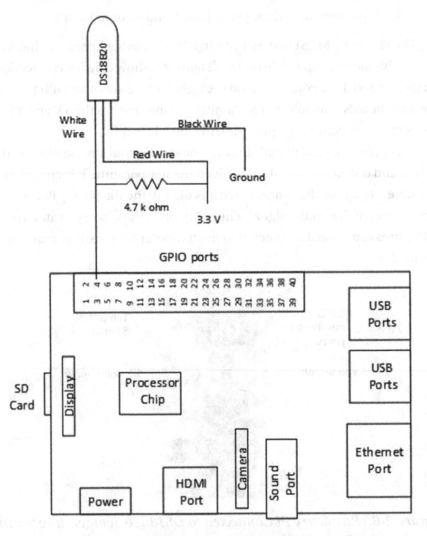

Figure 2-7. *Schematic of Temperature Sensor and Raspberry Pi*

The following link at Adafruit has a great example to connect a one-wire temperature sensor to a Raspberry Pi:

`https://learn.adafruit.com/adafruits-raspberry-pi-lesson-11-ds18b20-temperature-sensing`

One thing that is required is to set the Raspberry Pi configuration to one-wire. To do that, you need to open the terminal window and then type in the command sudo raspi-config to open the configuration tool described in Chapter 1. Then scroll down and select Interfacing Options which is 5. Another window will open and then scroll down to select one-wire. Select yes to enable and press Enter. In an older Raspberry Pi, you may need to use the Nano text editor to modify the config.txt file directly.

Listing 2-2 is the code used to scan the one-wire bus and capture the digital data sent to the Raspberry Pi.

Listing 2-2. Raspberry Pi Code PI_SN001 Basic 1 Wire Code

```
#PI_SN001_Basic_1wire
#Basic Pi one wire Temp sensor code
#Part 1 imports code modules
import glob
import time

#Part 2 Configures and opens the device
base_dir = '/sys/bus/w1/devices/'
device_folder = glob.glob(base_dir + '28*')[0]
device_file = device_folder + '/w1_slave'

def read_temp_raw():
    f = open(device_file, 'r')
    lines = f.readlines()
    f.close()
    return lines
```

```
#Part 3 reads the device data on the bus
def read_temp():
    lines = read_temp_raw()
    while lines[0].strip()[-3:] != 'YES':
        time.sleep(0.2)
        lines = read_temp_raw()
    equals_pos = lines[1].find('t=')
    if equals_pos != -1:
        temp_string = lines[1][equals_pos+2:]
        temp_c = float(temp_string) / 1000.0
        temp_f = temp_c * 9.0 / 5.0 + 32.0
        return temp_c, temp_f

#Part 4 prints the data in the monitor pane
while True:
    print(read_temp())

    time.sleep(1)
```

The preceding code consists of four parts that are labeled Parts 1, 2, 3, and 4. Part 1 imports the code modules that will be used. Part 2 configures the devices so the Raspberry Pi knows what is connected to the one-wire bus. Part 3 reads the device data, and then Part 4 records the value and sends it to the monitor pane running on the Raspberry Pi. In Part 3, the code takes the raw value and converts it to both degree Centigrade and Fahrenheit. The reader may notice the "#" symbol used in the code; this is a comment line and the computer ignores it. This is helpful to explain the code and document aspects.

To get it to run, go to Programming, open Python 3 or Thonny, find the file you saved it under, and open it.

Once in the program, select Run module, and then the data will start flowing.

Figure 2-8 shows how the code and data will look.

30

Figure 2-8. *Code Running and Capturing Data in Python 3 Development Tool*

The data on the left side can be highlighted and then copied over to a spreadsheet.

The authors also used the Thonny development tool (see Figure 2-9) which is both a compiler and debugger. A code debugger is a useful feature which lets the reader step through what the program has in memory for variables and really helps find flaws in the logic.

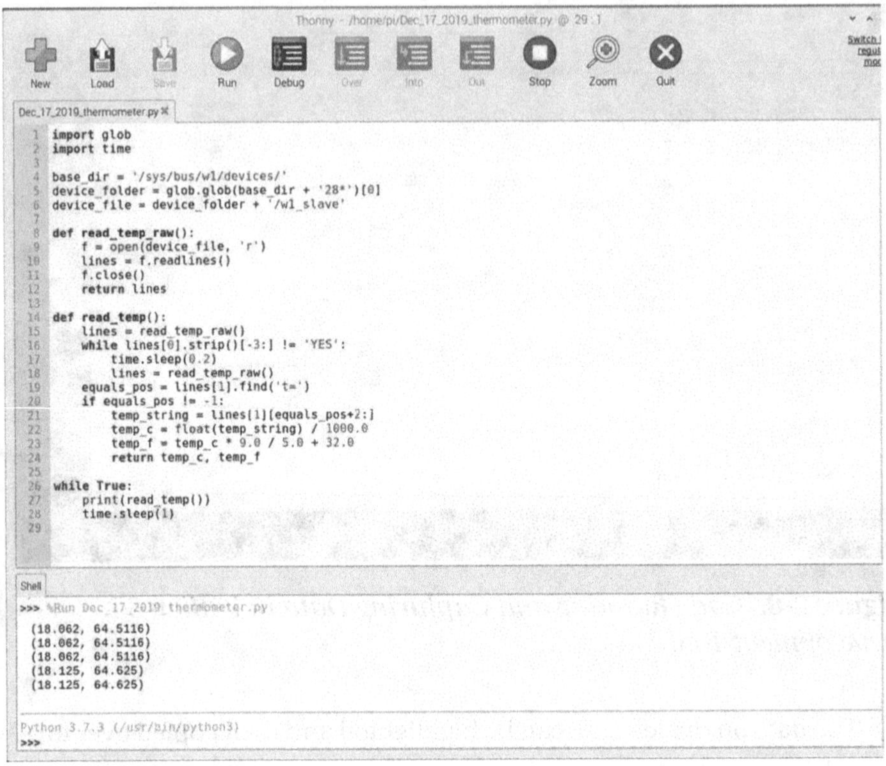

Figure 2-9. *Code Running and Capturing Data in Thonny Development Tool*

For readers who want to explore more about the Raspberry Pi and how it works with the one-wire devices and the I2C bus, this site has some good explanations and additional examples:

https://learn.sparkfun.com/tutorials/raspberry-pi-spi-and-i2c-tutorial/all

If the reader wants to create a data storage location, Listing 2-3 takes the data, creates a file if it does not exist, and then saves the data to the file. If there is a file, it just adds the data to it. This would provide a permanent record of the data if the reader is capturing a lot or if the Raspberry Pi is running unattended. This code is structured in a very similar fashion as Listing 2-2 and has very similar parts.

Note   Make sure The following bolded lines of code are on one line:

Listing 2-3.   Raspberry Pi Code PI_SN001B Advanced 1 Wire Code/ Data File

```
#Pi_SN001B
#Pi code to save data to file
#Code developed by Paul Bradt
import os
import glob
import time
from datetime import datetime
base_dir = '/sys/bus/w1/devices/'
device_folder = glob.glob(base_dir + '28*')[0]
device_file= device_folder + '/w1_slave'
sensor = 0
#To add a sensor need to change the number
def read_temp_raw():
    f = open(device_file, 'r')
    lines = f.readlines()
    f.close()
    return lines

def read_temp(sensor):
    lines = read_temp_raw()
    while lines[sensor].strip()[-3:] != 'YES':
        time.sleep(0.2)
        lines = read_temp_raw()
    equals_pos = lines[1].find('t=')
    if equals_pos != -1:
```

```
            temp_string = lines[1][equals_pos+2:]
            temp_c = float(temp_string) /  1000.0
            temp_f = temp_c * 9.0 / 5.0 + 32.0
            dt = datetime.now()
            sensor_Num = str(equals_pos) + " Sensor"
            return sensor_Num, dt.isoformat(), temp_c, temp_f
def main():
    while True:
        f= open("temp_sensor_readings_RevA.txt","a+")
        #a+ parameter tells open to append every time
        # the program runs.
        #Otherwise create a new file

        #Start a new for loop for each senosr here?

        lst_mixed = read_temp(sensor)
        #return as a tuple
        toWrite = ', '.join(str(x) for x in lst_mixed)
        #Add all the data from tuple into a single
        #string
        f.write(toWrite + "\n")
        print(toWrite)

        #f.write for file writing and print for
        #terminal.
        time.sleep(.3)

        f.close()
if __name__ == "__main__":
    main()
    #This is necessary to get the program to run
    #otherwise it will just execute
    #no code.run
```

The Arduino and the Raspberry Pi devices are approaching the *Star Trek* tricorder for gathering and saving data.

For those who really want to take this to the next level, this site describes a device built on a Raspberry Pi that resembles the *Star Trek* tricorder. It does not capture any data but instead plays videos of the original TV show; however, it looks incredible, and the Raspberry Pi fits inside the case:

`www.raspberrypi.org/blog/raspberry-pi-tricorder-prop/`

Summary

These projects point out some interesting aspects regarding the MCP9700 and DS18B20 sensors. First, the MCP9700 output is a linear relationship but requires an offset. The DS18B20 sensor is directly proportional to temperature. Another item observed is the comparison of the response time of the MCP9700 temp sensor and the DS18B20 waterproof temperature sensor. The DS18B20 is encased in a plastic cover and as such responds to temperature changes slower. This phenomenon is known as heat transfer and will be explored in later chapters. Finally, the MCP9700 is an analog sensor which means the millivolt reading is not modified or converted; it provides an analog output of the actual temperature. The DS18B20 is termed an I2C (Inter-Integrated Circuit) device where the raw voltage is converted over to a digital reading. This data can then be sent over a digital bus to the computer along with several other devices.

The Raspberry Pi is not set up to receive analog measurements, but with the addition of an analog to digital converter, it can accept this type of data. This is described in a later chapter. As the reader can see, there are advantages and disadvantages to both types of sensors. In a later chapter, there will be a third temperature sensor utilized. It is the LM35, and it will be in a different package that is sealed, designated TO. Electronically, it behaves very similar to the MCP9700.

While it is not necessary to complete these projects to proceed in this book, they lay the groundwork for using the Arduino and the Raspberry Pi tools to capture data. In particular, Listings 2-1 and 2-2 demonstrate the key sections of code that most of the code in this book follows. The reader should consider studying these examples to start to learn the language. When the Arduino IDE is downloaded, there is a folder created titled examples. In this folder, there are many pieces of code that provide a lot of useful examples. Studying these and other examples allows a researcher to start gathering data and then analyzing it or using it later. This groundwork will aid the reader when they develop their own or any of the other remaining projects.

CHAPTER 3

Physics and Mathematics Basics

This chapter covers a few basic areas of physics and mathematics that are important for science and engineering, namely, temperature, force, pressure, and some general algebra/statistics concepts. Why are these areas so important? Because they govern the physical world and how many things work or behave. Understanding of these tools can provide the background to ways of improving life, increasing energy efficiency, improving products, increasing safety, and other innumerable facets of life.

Temperature

Temperature is a measure of a physical property of all matter, and it represents a level of internal energy the object or material contains. Another way of looking at temperature is a comparison of energy levels within or between objects or materials. For example, a hot object has more internal energy than a cold object. In theory, at a temperature of absolute zero, there is no energy.

There are two temperature scales (English and Metric) used, and they have both a full-scale component and a scale that is used for everyday temperature measurements. The following equations highlight various conversions of 32 degrees Fahrenheit or the freezing point of water to other temperature scales:

© Paul Bradt and David Bradt 2020
P. Bradt and D. Bradt, *Science and Engineering Projects Using the Arduino and Raspberry Pi*,
https://doi.org/10.1007/978-1-4842-5811-8_3

Fahrenheit (°F) to Rankine (°R):

32°F + 459.67 = 491.67°R

Fahrenheit to Celsius:

(32°F − 32) × 5/9 = 0°C

Celsius (°C) to Kelvin (°K):

0°C + 273.15 = 273.15°K

Temperature is a key measure in how weather works and plays a significant role in our comfort. It is amazing how we are heating or cooling our home, to control its temperature, sometimes doing both in the same day!

Force

What does force really mean and why is it critical to everything we do?

An object will not move from a state of rest unless a force acts upon it. Putting it simply, no movement occurs unless a force is generated by some means, and that force pushes or pulls an object. For example, as a baby learns to walk, she gains a very real lesson on how to control all facets of force and balance in order to get from the table to her mother. As she starts out, she must pay attention to the force needed to move forward. Otherwise, she may lose her balance and fall down. If the floor is slippery and she fails to keep her weight over her feet, she may not be able to keep from slipping and will fall down. If she does not keep moving and slows down, she may not be able to keep her balance, and she falls down. Over time we do these things without consciously thinking about them and are able to walk from point A to point B without incident. These basic constraints are inescapable and continually govern many aspects of our daily life.

Pressure

It is the measure of a uniform force over a given area. Figure 3-1 illustrates a force (F), spread uniformly over a known area (A). Given that an unchanging force is exerted on a surface, a reduction in surface area would result in an increase in pressure and, conversely, a decrease in pressure if the surface area were enlarged.

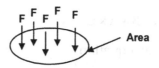

**Pressure is Force exerted
over an area**

***Figure 3-1.** Diagram Showing Pressure*

Pressure = Force/Area, abbreviated as P=F/A

Metric system: Pressure = N/m² (Newton per square meter)

English system: Pressure = lbs/in² or psi (pounds per sq. inch)

Why is pressure important? It is a measure of true exerted force. An experiment later in the book shows how changing the surface area can really change the force an object experiences. Think about when an apple is being cut. When the point of the knife is poked through the skin, the applied pressure at the point of the knife is very high. However, it is very hard to cut through the skin of an apple using the whole length of the blade.

Basic Concept of Algebra

Algebra's fundamental concept is the manipulation of equations moving the variables around to solve for a specific variable or establish relationships of interest. Here are some key algebraic tools:

Distributive property

Multiplying A by the expression in the parenthesis:

$A \times (B + C) = A \times B + A \times C$

Manipulating an equation

A variable can be subtracted from or added to both sides of the equation:

If $A + B = C + D + B$

subtracting B from both sides yields

$A = C + D$

Also, a variable can be multiplied or divided on both sides of the equation:

$7 \times A = B$

Then dividing by 7 on both sides yields

$A = B/7$

While these operations seem simple, they form the basis of setting up equations to solve many different variables. Using these operations provides a number of ways to resolve and answer many scientific or engineering questions.

Statistical Concepts

The authors do not go into great detail regarding statistics in this book, but this section is included to highlight some important basics of this important tool. Statistics is a method that is used to analyze the variability of data and research meaningful trends of large groups of data.

Arithmetic mean or average: Calculated by dividing the sum of a set of values by the quantity of those values.

$$X_{average} = (X1+X2+X3+...)/\text{quantity of values of X}$$

Standard deviation (Std Dev): A measure of the variance about the mean.

$$\text{Std Dev} = \text{Square root of } (1/N \times \sum((X_i - \text{Mean})^2))$$

What is happening in the standard deviation equation? For each value, a difference is found from the mean value. Those differences are squared and summed, and finally the square root of that number is found. What is this actually telling us? The equation establishes a value for an expected "deviation" from the mean. When the analyst is looking at additional data gathered and sees a significant difference in standard deviation, it may indicate there is a problem somewhere.

Statistics is a very complex subject, and the preceding concepts are the basics. They do provide the groundwork for most of statistical analysis. If the reader is exploring a scientific or engineering career, they are encouraged to explore statistics in greater detail, in particular, hypothesis testing.

Direct Compared to Inferred Measurements

A direct measurement is a measure of the item of interest. An example of a direct measurement is a voltmeter measuring voltage. An example of an inferred measurement is when another aspect is measured and the item of interest is inferred from what can be measured. In many cases, the sensors in this book like the MCP9700 transistor temperature sensor actually provide an output voltage based on the temperature at the sensor. The temperature is an inferred measurement.

Summary

The world is a very unique place, and the concepts outlined in this chapter provide the basics of some of the most important engineering tools and scientific concepts. The reader is encouraged to explore them further in later chapters along with advanced classes and studies.

CHAPTER 4

Simple Science and Engineering Projects

This chapter explains several simple science and engineering projects that can provide data on some basic physical properties. These are good projects to explore science, engineering, the Arduino, and the Raspberry Pi. These projects can be useful too. The first project is a small-scale version of a key driving mechanism of how weather works. The second project highlights aspects of force and pressure including how distributing force over a different area changes the applied pressure. The final project is an automated tool to capture the number of events happening over time. This could be useful capturing scientific data, for example, examining the number of meteorites during a shower or the number of lightning strikes during a thunderstorm. These tools are great for measuring and observing key scientific concepts. Fortunately, the engineering skills and techniques needed to build these projects is relatively easy.

Buoyancy of Air

The first project will use two temperature sensors to track temperature change in two different elevations inside a house. It will demonstrate that hot air rises and the effect of buoyancy.

P. Bradt and D. Bradt, *Science and Engineering Projects Using the Arduino and Raspberry Pi*, https://doi.org/10.1007/978-1-4842-5811-8_4

43

Science   Buoyancy of heated air and using one form of the ideal gas law.

Technology/Engineering   Using the Arduino or the Raspberry Pi and temperature sensors to collect data, to test methods, and to improve temperature distribution in a house.

Mathematics   This section explores the mathematics associated with density changes of air as a function of temperature. As air heats up and energy is added, the density decreases, and it will float on the colder denser air. If it is cooled, it will sink.

The mathematics associated with this project uses these variables with the goal of calculating the change of density based on temperature changes:

P = Pressure

ρ = Density

T = Temperature

R = Specific gas constant

$\rho = P/(R \times T)$

As can be seen in the preceding equation, if the temperature (T) increases and the pressure is held close to constant, then the density will decrease which causes the warmer gas to rise. On a larger scale, the sun warms the Earth's atmosphere, which causes a large mass of air density to decrease. This movement may result in winds and breezes. Enough of a temperature change and the pressure may decrease which will cause more wind flowing from high-pressure areas to low-pressure areas.

Arduino Buoyancy of Air Version

This project is similar to the Arduino project in Chapter 2; however, it uses libraries and the I2C temperature sensor used in the Raspberry Pi data logging project. The code is a little more complex and uses libraries which are ready-to-use packages of code that are called up when needed. These significantly simplify the code needed. The user will need to download the required libraries onto their computer in the library folder.

From an engineering perspective, these are the parts shown in Figure 4-1 that are needed to build the Arduino version of this project:

- Arduino Uno 3

- 2 DS18B20 waterproof temperature sensors

- 4.7K Ω resistor

- Miscellaneous wires, proto-board, and terminal strips

- One piece of wood to mount the components on

Figure 4-1. *Arduino and Two I2C Temperatures Sensors*

Figure 4-2 shows how the sensors were placed in the house to get the two readings. Figure 4-3 is the schematic showing how to connect them to the Arduino.

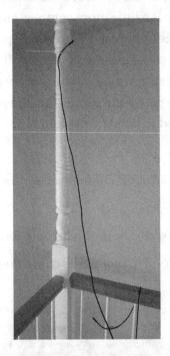

Figure 4-2. *Two Temperature Sensors*

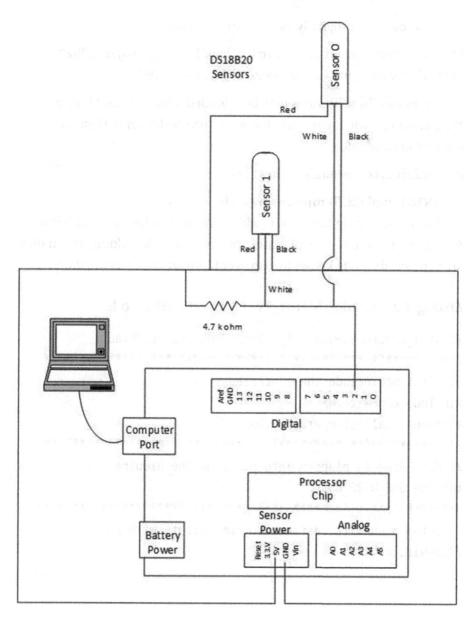

Figure 4-3. *Arduino and Two One-Wire Temperature Sensors*

This code was originally found at this web site:

```
https://create.arduino.cc/projecthub/TheGadgetBoy/ds18b20-
digital-temperature-sensor-and-arduino-9cc806
```

It requires these libraries to b downloaded: One Wire and Dallas Temperature. If you are not familiar with Arduino libraries, then this site has a lot of good info:

```
www.arduino.cc/en/guide/libraries
```

SN103 Dual I2C Temp Sensors code

The comments in Listing 4-1 (which are either after two // or between /* and */) provide good explanation of what the code is doing. When these are in place, the code knows to skip over them and not execute them.

Listing 4-1. Arduino SN103_Two Sensors 1 Wire Code

```
//SN103_1_wire_2sensors_8_3_2019 Modified by PBradt
/******************************************************/
// First we include the libraries
#include <OneWire.h>
#include <DallasTemperature.h>
/******************************************************/
// Data wire is plugged into pin 2 on the Arduino
#define ONE_WIRE_BUS 2
/******************************************************/
// Setup a oneWire instance to communicate with any
//OneWire devices
```

```
// (not just Maxim/Dallas temperature ICs)
OneWire oneWire(ONE_WIRE_BUS);
/*******************************************************/
// OneWire reference to Dallas Temperature.
DallasTemperature sensors(&oneWire);
/*******************************************************/
void setup(void)
{
 // start serial port
 Serial.begin(9600);
 Serial.println("Dallas Control Library");

 Serial.println("This is SN103");

 // Start up the library
 sensors.begin();
}
void loop(void)
{
 // call sensors.requestTemperatures()
 // to all devices on the bus
/*******************************************************/
 Serial.print(" Requesting temperatures...");
 sensors.requestTemperatures();
// Send the command to get temperature readings
 Serial.println("DONE");
/*******************************************************/
 Serial.print("Temperature0 is: ");
 Serial.print(sensors.getTempCByIndex(0));
 Serial.println("");
 Serial.print("Temperature1 is: ");
 Serial.print(sensors.getTempCByIndex(1));
```

```
Serial.println("");
// You can have more than one DS18B20 on the same
//bus.
   // 0 refers to the first IC on the wire
   delay(10000);
}
```

Data was taken on a warm day, and it shows when the air conditioner is running, there is a lot of mixing of the air and the temperature equalizes out over time.

Temp 0 is 20 inches (0.5 m) from the ceiling.

Temp 1 is about 24 inches (0.6 m) from the floor.

The room is 8 feet high (2.4 m).

The distance between the sensors is 2.4 − (0.5 +0.6) = 1.3 m.

This is SN103

Requesting temperatures...13:18:33.593 -> DONE

13:18:33.593 -> Temperature0 is: 24.87

13:18:33.640 -> Temperature1 is: 24.19

13:18:43.696 -> Requesting temperatures...DONE

13:18:44.446 -> Temperature0 is: 24.81

13:18:44.446 -> Temperature1 is: 24.19

13:18:54.501 -> Requesting temperatures...DONE

13:18:55.276 -> Temperature0 is: 24.69

13:18:55.276 -> Temperature1 is: 24.19

13:19:05.331 -> Requesting temperatures...DONE

13:19:06.081 -> Temperature0 is: 24.56

13:19:06.128 -> Temperature1 is: 24.19

13:19:16.183 -> Requesting temperatures...DONE

13:19:16.932 -> Temperature0 is: 24.50

13:19:16.932 -> Temperature1 is: 24.12

13:19:26.996 -> Requesting temperatures...DONE

13:19:27.746 -> Temperature0 is: 24.37

13:19:27.793 -> Temperature1 is: 24.12

13:19:37.803 -> Requesting temperatures...DONE

13:19:38.553 -> Temperature0 is: 24.31

13:19:38.600 -> Temperature1 is: 24.12

13:19:48.633 -> Requesting temperatures...DONE

13:19:49.383 -> Temperature0 is: 24.25

13:19:49.430 -> Temperature1 is: 24.19

13:19:59.475 -> Requesting temperatures...DONE

13:20:00.213 -> Temperature0 is: 24.25

13:20:00.260 -> Temperature1 is: 24.12

13:20:10.320 -> Requesting temperatures...DONE

13:20:11.069 -> Temperature0 is: 24.19

13:20:11.069 -> Temperature1 is: 24.19

Calculation of density and summary of the data:

$\rho = P/(R \times T)$

The starting Temperature0 of 24.87 °C is 298.02 °K.

The starting Temperature1 of 24.19 °C is 297.34 °K.

The specific gas constant for dry air is 287.058 J/ (kg·K) in SI unit

or 8.314462618 m3·Pa·K−1·mol−1.

Calculating the density and assuming a constant volume At 20 °C and 101.325 kPa pressure at the two temperatures yields the results below:

Density at T_0 = P/(R x T) = 101325/(8.314462618 x 298.02) =

40.89.

Density at T_1 = P/(R x T) = 101325/(8.314462618 x 297.34) =

40.99.

The preceding calculations show that at T_0 the air is approximately 0.24% less dense than at T_1; therefore, that piece of air will rise and float on top of the colder dense air. Once the air conditioner blows the air around, it pushes colder air down, but eventually there is enough mixing that the temperature between the two locations mixes and evens out.

Raspberry Pi Buoyancy of Air Version

This project uses the Raspberry Pi and the LM35 temperature sensor to also capture the temperature difference at two heights in a house. One other item that is needed is an analog to digital converter (ADC). This is needed because the LM35 sensor is an analog device, but the Raspberry Pi only accepts digital inputs.

The parts needed are

- Raspberry Pi 3

- MCM 40-pin GPIO breakout board and cable for Raspberry Pi (or equivalent)

- 2 LM35 sensors that are connected to a wire harness (see Appendix)

- MCP3008 analog to digital converter (ADC)

- Miscellaneous wires, proto-board, and terminal strips

The authors found a lot of confusing information online regarding the use of the Raspberry Pi and the MCP3008 ADC. They found the following code which works well as long as its SPI configuration matches the pins on the Raspberry Pi. One of the confusing aspects in the documentation on the Internet regarding connecting to the ADC is the connections to GPIO. There are four key connections and multiple designations. The first one is pin number 23. This is also designated GPIO11 and the SPI SCLK clock connection. The next key connection is pin 24, and its other designations are GPIO8 and SPI CE0 or chip enable. Another key connection is pin number 19, also designated GPIO10 or SPI MOSI. The final key connection is pin number 21, also designated GPIO9 or SPI MISO. Keeping these key connections in mind and understanding the multiple designations will help to ensure the reader will get this powerful tool connected and running. The MCP3008 ADC can accept up to eight sensor inputs.

Figure 4-4 shows the assembled unit with the MCM 40-pin GPIO breakout board and the MCP 3008 ADC.

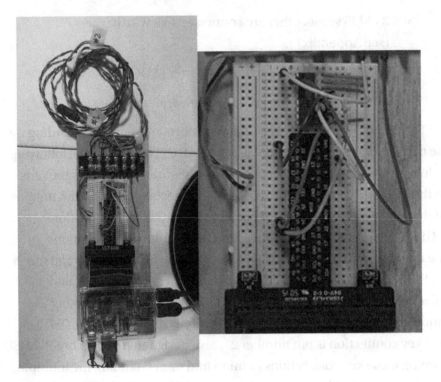

Figure 4-4. *Raspberry Pi Setup to Measure Air Temperature*

Figure 4-5 shows the sensor assembled to a small circuit board and then the heat shrink tubing placed over it to insulate and protect the device from inadvertent shorts of the wires.

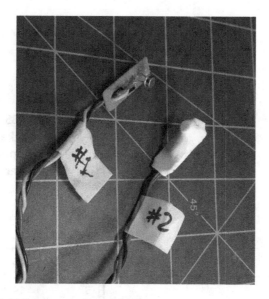

Figure 4-5. *LM35 Sensor Assemblies*

Figure 4-6 is the schematic that shows how to connect the Raspberry Pi with the ADC and then the LM35 temperature sensors.

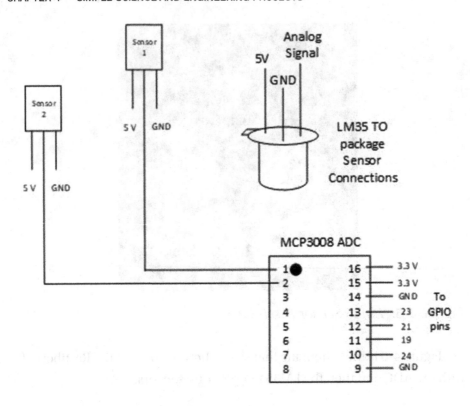

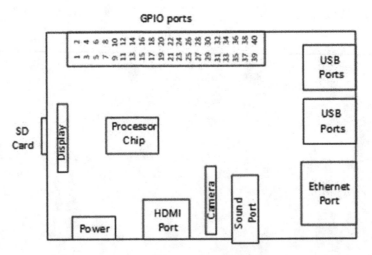

Figure 4-6. *Raspberry Pi, A to D Converter, and Two LM35 Sensors*

The basis for this code (Listing 4-2) was found on this Raspberry Pi web site. There is a bit of discussion regarding A to D converters that the reader might find helpful:

www.raspberrypi.org/forums/viewtopic.php?t=221972

Note   The five lines of bold code below are each on one line in the program:

Listing 4-2. Raspberry Pi Code PI_SN002A Two Analog Temperature Sensors

```
#Pi_SN002A
# Simple example of reading the MCP3008 analog input # channels
# Convert to Temperature.
# Original code from Author: Tony DiCola
# Modified by Paul Bradt

# License: Public Domain
import time

# Import SPI library (for hardware SPI) and MCP3008
# library.
import Adafruit_GPIO.SPI as SPI
import Adafruit_MCP3008

# Software SPI configuration:
CLK  = 23
```

```python
CS   = 24
MISO = 21
MOSI = 19
mcp = Adafruit_MCP3008.MCP3008(clk=CLK, cs=CS, miso=MISO, mosi=MOSI)

# Hardware SPI configuration:
# SPI_PORT   = 0
# SPI_DEVICE = 0
# mcp = Adafruit_MCP3008.MCP3008(spi=SPI.SpiDev(SPI_PORT, SPI_DEVICE))

print('Reading MCP3008 values')
# Print nice channel column headers.
print('| {0:>4} | {1:>4} | {2:>4} | {3:>4} | {4:>4} | {5:>4} |
{6:>4} | {7:>4} |'.format(*range(8)))
#print('-' * 57)

# Main program loop.
while True:
    # Read all the ADC channel values in a list.
    values = [0]*8
    for i in range(8):
        # The read_adc function will get the value of # the
        # specified channel (0-7).
        values[i] = mcp.read_adc(i)
    #Math for converting raw digital value into F/C
    #Temperatures
    values[2] = values[0]/1023.0*330.0
    values[3] = values[1]/1023.0*330.0
    values[4] = (values[2]*9/5+32)
    values[5] = (values[3]*9/5+32)
```

```
print('| {0:>2} Raw 1| {1:>2} Raw 2| {2:>2} C for 1| {3:>2}
C for 2| {4:>2} F for 1| {5:>2} F for 2|'.format(*values))
# Pause for half a second.
time.sleep(0.5)
```

The Raspberry Pi version provides another way to gather data to observe and monitor buoyancy of air, temperature changes, and how well the air mixes when the air conditioning is turned on.

Buoyancy Recap

These two projects explore ways of demonstrating and capturing buoyancy of air data and provide a way to track temperatures in two different heights in a room. This can be utilized to observe how air mixes and evens out the temperature when an air conditioner or fan is running. Additionally, it may be helpful assessing the benefits of ceiling fans and other ways to improve a home's environment.

Demonstrating Pressure

This next project will help to clear up some of the confusion that may exist between force and pressure. They are related, and the mathematics showing this relationship will be demonstrated. The system in this project uses a force sensor to demonstrate how to measure force and applied pressure on a force sensor. It also demonstrates the concept of distributing a load over different areas. This concept of changing loads by changing the area is key to many civil and mechanical engineering problems.

Science   Gain an understanding of the difference between the principles of pressure and force.

Technology/Engineering   Using the Arduino and a force sensor.

Mathematics   Converting the sensor voltage reading to pressure based on the sensor's calibration.

The parts needed are

- Arduino Uno 3

- Square force sensor resistor (Adafruit or SparkFun)

- 10K Ω resistor

- Miscellaneous wires, proto-board, and terminal strips

- Several pieces of wood and a stack of ten pennies (or other coins)

Adafruit has a very good description of how this force sensor works along with a calibration curve showing where it is linear and indicating where it is not. The discussion on this site is that the force sensor is not an accurate device; however, it can be used to gain insight from relative force comparisons, in other words, comparing one measurement to another.

The Appendix section shows the technique needed to solder the wires to the force sensor.

Figure 4-7 shows an Arduino connected to the force sensor along with the stack of pennies sitting on top of a square piece of wood on the force sensor.

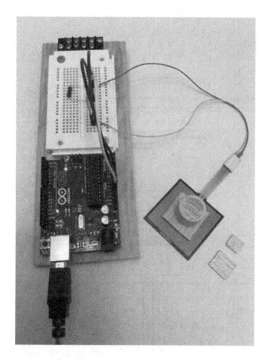

Figure 4-7. *Measuring Force with Arduino*

Figure 4-8 shows the schematic to connect the force sensor to the Arduino. The resistor is part of a voltage divider and is compared to the sensor's resistance.

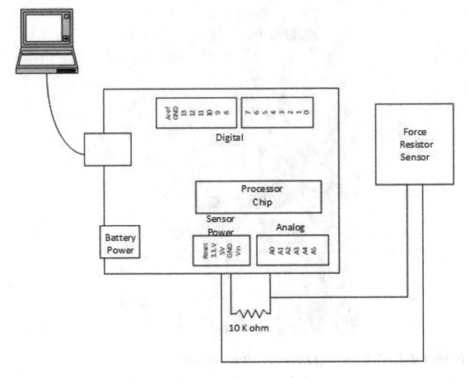

Figure 4-8. *Schematic of Force Measurement*

The basic sketch or Arduino code contains four primary elements:

1. The first step of the program is to set up the variables.

2. The program sets up the serial port communication rate.

3. The program runs a repeating loop that cleans registers and then gets new data.

4. The Arduino sends data to the serial port on the computer.

Listing 4-3 is the code, and it reads the data from the sensor and then sends it over the serial line to the computer.

Note   The follwoing bold line of code needs to be on one line in the IDE:

Listing 4-3. Arduino SN104_Basic Force Sensor Code

```
//SN104 Force Sensor Basic Code
//From the article: http://bildr.org/2012/11/force-//sensitive-
resistor-arduino

int FSR_Pin = A0; //analog pin 0

void setup(){
  Serial.begin(9600);
}

void loop(){
  int FSRReading = analogRead(FSR_Pin);

  Serial.println(FSRReading);
  delay(5000);
  //delay(100); //Use this delay for zero g
  //Count is in msec adjust here to slow down the
  //output for easier reading
}
```

For those who want to modify and improve the code, the following is an example of how you might convert the direct reading from the sensor to pressure. The factors and size of the interface may need to be adjusted based on what the researcher uses. This code uses the double function which is needed when the Arduino is doing detailed calculations.

This modified code (Listing 4-4) converts the output to a pressure reading of pounds per square inch.

Note   The code that is bold below is on one line and should not overwrap when typed into the IDE.

Listing 4-4. Arduino Code SN104B Force Sensor Pressure Calculation

```
//SN104B Force Sensor and Pressure Calculation Code
//From the article: http://bildr.org/2012/11/force-//sensitive-
resistor-arduino
//Code Modified by Paul Bradt
int FSR_Pin = A0; //analog pin 0
int FSRReading;
double AnalogRatio = 44;
double weight = .055;
double area = 1.0;
double PSIresult;

void setup(){
  Serial.begin(9600);

  //Example code to convert the sensor readings with
  //area and weight you measure for
  // Pressure (in PSI) calculation.
}

void loop(){
  FSRReading = analogRead(FSR_Pin);
  PSIresult = 0;

  PSIresult = (double)( FSRReading / AnalogRatio * weight / area );

  Serial.print("FSR analog read is: ");
  Serial.println(FSRReading);
  Serial.print("PSI result is: ");
  Serial.println(PSIresult);
  delay(5000);
  //Count is in msec
  //adjust to slow down the output for easier reading
}
```

The data in Table 4-1 shows the relationship between the force reading and how it changes if it is distributed over different areas.

Table 4-1. *Analysis of the Data from Force Sensor Measurements*

Test	Side of Area Interface (inches)	Area (square inches)	Average Voltage Reading	¼ of Voltage Reading
1	1	1	44.8	N/A
2	0.5	0.25	159.5	40
3	0.25	0.0625	327.75	82

For example, use Test 1 as the basis for comparison. The Test 2 area is ¼ of Test 1 (4 × 0.25 = 1). So the same force is pushing on ¼ the area, and the sensor would see four times the force. If we divide the reading of Test 2 by 4, we get very close to the Test 1 reading. This is in the last column of Table 4-1. For Test 3, the relationship breaks down; this may have to do with the sensitivity of the sensor for this small area.

Pressure/Force Recap

This project demonstrates and clarifies the difference between pressure and force. It demonstrates a very important concept showing how the applied load can be reduced by changing the area where the force interacts.

Capturing Counts

Scientists often need to count occurrences of events and compare them between different hypotheses. This project will show how to capture very fast events and count them to monitor the number of occurrences. Some examples might be meteorites or lightning strikes. When things happen very fast and there is not enough time to mark down an event on paper, this project allows the reader to just push a button and record these events.

Science   If there is a need to count events to understand probability and likelihood of scientific data.

Technology/Engineering   Using the Arduino and a pushbutton switch.

Mathematics   Aspects of statistics can be utilized to understand likelihood of data of event occurrence.

The parts needed are

- Arduino Uno 3

- Pushbutton switch

- 10K Ω resistor

- Miscellaneous wires, proto-board, and terminal strips

- Old-style 35 mm file canister to hold the remote switch

The right side of Figure 4-9 shows the inside of the old-style 35 mm film canister with the pushbutton mounted there. The cap is fastened to the board and then a notch cut out for the wires to pass through. This provides a nice grip to hold so the observer can focus on watching for events. The left side of Figure 4-9 shows the switch connected to the Arduino.

Figure 4-9. *Using the Arduino to Capture Count of Events*

Figure 4-10 is the schematic showing how to connect the pushbutton switch to the Arduino.

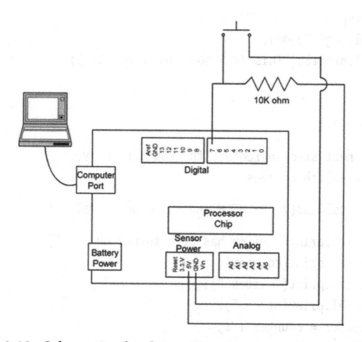

Figure 4-10. *Schematic of Arduino Counting Events*

Listing 4-5 is the code, and it is somewhat basic but captures the number of times a switch has been pushed, after which it sends that info over the serial port to the computer.

Listing 4-5. Arduino SN105 Capturing Counts Code

```
//SN105_Counts_Nov_2019
//Code developed by Paul and David Bradt

int counter = 0;
//Program uses Switch to set high state and
//increments count holds high until it changes to low state.
```

```
//Sends count increment over serial line

bool switchOn = false;

void setup() {
  Serial.begin(9600);
  Serial.println("This is SN105 counts events");

}

void loop() {

  //The next step increments the counter every
  //time switch changes

  if(digitalRead(7) == HIGH and switchOn == false){

    Serial.print("Switch has been turned on for ");
    Serial.print(counter);
    Serial.print(" times.");
    Serial.println("    ");
    counter = counter + 1;
    switchOn = true;

  //Delay ensures switch does not bounce
    delay(500);
  }

  //The next step determines switch state
  if(digitalRead(7) == LOW and switchOn == true){

    switchOn = false;
  }
}
```

Some example data is captured and shown in Figure 4-11 using the serial port and the time stamp activated.

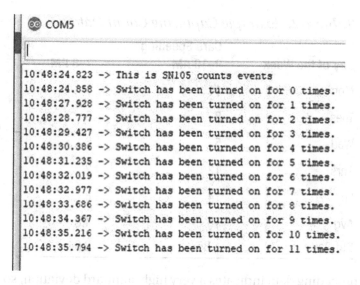

Figure 4-11. *Screen Capture of Data from Arduino Count of Events*

How could this setup be utilized? Assume there are two similar events where the counts of occurrences need to be analyzed, for example, the number of cars that appear to be traveling over the speed limit on a road. In one time slot from 9 to 10 AM, there are 11 cars found speeding, but there are only 5 speeding between 7 and 8 PM. This data is collected for the rest of the week and is listed in Table 4-2. The street is not in a school zone, but it is close to a school. This analysis could help with the comparison of how drivers react to the knowledge that they are driving near a school zone when a reduction in speed is required.

Table 4-2. *Example Capturing Count Data*

Day of the Week	Cars Speeding 9–10 AM	7–8 PM
Mon	11	5
Tues	8	3
Wed	5	6
Thrs	12	2
Fri	14	8
Avg	10	4.8
Std Dev	4.85	2.64

The preceding data indicates a very high standard deviation, so we may need more data to see if there is a better correlation or it may just vary that high and be somewhat unpredictable.

Counts Recap

This tool can be used to capture several different types of events. If the switch is not the best input device, there are other types of sensors like infrared sensors that could be used to track fast events. The data can then be analyzed using statistics of event occurrence, and this type of analysis is key to many scientific studies.

Summary

The projects in this chapter provide tools to measure and analyze some key scientific parameters. These include air temperature buoyancy which is a primary driver in the weather of the world. The next project shows how to measure pressure and how area impacts this value given the same force. This is key to distributing load and a very important factor in many engineering projects. Finally, the last project provides a tool to quickly capture event occurrence and can be used to accurately obtain the number of events of interest for statistical analysis.

CHAPTER 5

Advanced Physics and Mathematics for Science and Engineering

This chapter elaborates on some advanced topics of mathematics and how they can be used to model aspects that are time dependent. Included in this chapter are descriptions of some basic and more advanced mathematical aspects of calculus, heat transfer, velocity, acceleration, and integration. Other physical aspects related to mass, friction, inertia, and momentum are discussed. This is a lot to cover, and this text scratches the surface; however, with these key concepts, the reader will understand many factors that dominate our environment.

There are several equations in this chapter that model or simulate reality. There is a brief explanation for each, and many will be used in later projects in this book to explain and demonstrate how the equation can be utilized to model reality.

© Paul Bradt and David Bradt 2020
P. Bradt and D. Bradt, *Science and Engineering Projects Using the Arduino and Raspberry Pi*,
https://doi.org/10.1007/978-1-4842-5811-8_5

Basics Terms of Calculus

Calculus is the mathematical method that deals with the relationship of a change between two or more variables. Some examples include speed or velocity which is the change of distance over the change of time. Calculus uses standard symbols to represent these changes, normally a lower case d with the variable of interest (change in distance x is written as dx). The small letter d is utilized to represent the Greek letter delta or the change in a value. The following equations show and expand on relationships of heat transfer, velocity, acceleration, and other items.

How Heat Transfer Works

How does temperature affect heat transfer? One can gain a better understanding of heat transfer by looking at temperature as the driving force that causes heat (or energy) to move from a hot object or area to a cooler object or area. It is analogous to the water system in your house. Opening a water faucet introduces a low pressure to the system, and the high pressure within the water pipes pushes water out the faucet to the ambient low-pressure zone. This represents the tendency of any system with varying energy levels to become uniform...to equalize over time. Heat energy responds to this tendency toward uniformity through three primary transfer methods called conduction, convection, and radiation. The equations for heat transfer came from resource [3].

Conduction Heat Transfer

Conduction heat transfer occurs inside a solid object. Conduction heat transfer is heat that moves through an object with almost no movement of the object's particles. Another way to look at conduction heat transfer is each particle within the object receives heat from the particle next to it and then passes it to the next particle and so on throughout the object.

Figure 5-1 illustrates this concept by showing how heat is transferred through a rod from the hot end to the cold end.

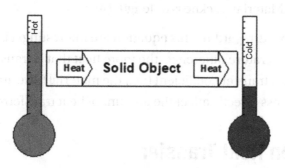

Figure 5-1. *Conduction Heat Transfer*

Different materials transfer heat at different rates. The factor that is used to calculate the amount of heat transfer rates in materials is called the conduction heat transfer coefficient. Metals tend to have high conduction heat transfer coefficients, while insulators and plastics tend to have low conduction heat transfer coefficients. See the Appendix for a list of thermal conductivity coefficients for various materials. Unless more energy is put into the object over time, the temperature will equalize, and the heat transfer rate will eventually go to zero. The following equation is the basic equation for heat transfer via conduction:

$$dq/dt = (k \, dA \, (T_h - T_c))/dx$$

This equation shows that the temperature difference, the area, and the length of the object are driving factors in the amount of heat transferred via conduction
where

dq/dt = Heat transfer over time (Joule/sec).

k = Conduction heat transfer coefficient (Joule/sec-m-C°). This is material dependent.

dA = Area through which heat is transferred (m²).

Th = Temperature at hot location (C°).

Tc = Temperature at cold location (C°).

dx = Material thickness or length (m).

Several aspects regarding this equation are interesting. First, the greater the temperature difference, the more heat that is transferred. Second, the heat transfer coefficient (i.e., the material), the area, and the material thickness directly affect the amount of heat transferred.

Convection Heat Transfer

Convection heat transfer is caused by the movement of a fluid or gas from one area to another area. This movement of a fluid over a surface is the primary difference between conduction and convection. Figure 5-2 demonstrates convection heat transfer in a fluid or gas.

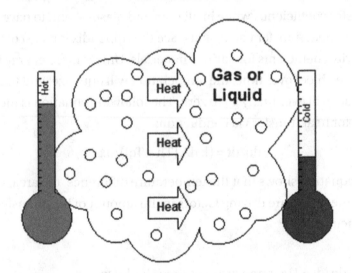

Figure 5-2. *Convection Heat Transfer*

One example of convection heat transfer is how hot air rises. A good demonstration is how a hot-air balloon captures the rising hot air when the burner is turned on. When a heat source warms the air around it, that air rises (this was demonstrated as buoyancy in the previous chapter). This brings in cooler air from around that area, and then the cooler air is warmed. The net result is heat is transferred upward because warm air is more buoyant because it is less dense. This is called natural convection. Natural convection in a fireplace continually feeds oxygen to the fire.

Another form of convection heat transfer is forced convection. In this case, a fluid or gas is forced to flow over a surface. The temperature difference between the fluid and the surface transfers the heat. Forced convection can be used to cool a hot object, for example, when you turn a fan on and the air blows across your skin cooling you. Forced convection can also be used to heat an object. An example of this is how the heater in your car blows warm air into the car to warm the driver and passengers.

The next equation is the basic equation for heat transfer by natural convection:

$$dq/dt = h \, dA \, (Th - Tc)$$

This equation shows that the temperature difference and the area are driving factors in the amount of heat transferred via natural convection where

dq/dt = Heat transfer (Joule/secs).

h = Surface convection heat transfer coefficient (Joule/sec-m^2-$C°$). The value of this variable can become very complex to determine as it is dependent on the gas, the conditions on the surface, the temperature, humidity, velocity of flow across it, and other items.

dA = Area through which heat is transferred (m^2).

Th = Temperature at hot location ($C°$).

Tc = Temperature at cold location ($C°$).

Radiation Heat Transfer

The term radiation as it is used in heat transfer is different than its normal use. It does not necessarily result from a nuclear reaction, but it does require a very hot object. The object is so hot that it actually gives off energy in the form of light, and the light is the medium that transfers the energy. Figure 5-3 demonstrates this concept where the light from the sun carries heat through the cold of space all the way to Earth. That light warms our planet.

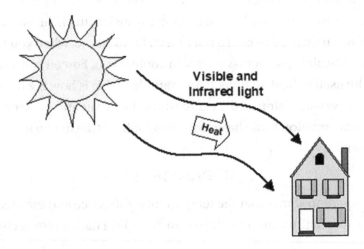

Figure 5-3. *Heat Transfer by Radiation*

The factors that impact heat transfer by radiation are temperature and the surface of the material absorbing the heat. The next equation describes heat transfer by radiation:

$$dq/dt = \varepsilon \, 6 \, A \, (T1^4 - T2^4)$$

This equation shows that the temperature difference is the primary factor in radiation heat transfer because they are raised to the fourth power where dq/dt = Heat transfer (Joule/secs).

ε = Emissivity is a factor of the material and indicates how much of the energy is emitted due to the internal temperature.

6 = Stefan-Boltzmann constant = $5.67 \times 10\text{-}8 \ W/m^2 - K^4$.

A = Area through which heat is transferred (m^2).

T1 = Temperature at hot location (°K).

T2 = Temperature at cold location (°K).

Using the preceding equation, it can be shown that approximately 1000 W/m^2 reaches the Earth's surface on a sunny day. Most of the energy of light resides in the infrared and visible spectrum.

This amount of energy must be adjusted given the angle at which the sunrays hit the Earth's surface. The following equation can be used to calculate the amount of heat reaching the Earth's surface due to the angle Θ of the light striking the Earth:

$$dq/dt = (1000 \ W/m^2) \ \epsilon \ A \cos \Theta$$

where Θ = the angle of the solar rays as they strike the object.

All Three Heat Transfer Mechanisms Work Together!

In many cases, there may be two or three heat transfer mechanisms occurring at the same time. For example, when a pot is put on an electric stove and the heating element is on high, all three mechanisms are at work. The pot is in direct contact with the stove heating element, so conduction is at work. The air around the stove heating element is warmed, so it rises around the pot transferring heat via convection. Finally, if the stove heating element is on high, it most likely will be glowing red and hot enough to give off heat via radiation. It is straightforward to calculate the total heat transferred. Simply add each value for conduction, convection, and radiation. However, in many cases, one heat transfer mechanism dominates, and the others can be neglected.

The researcher should keep in mind that this summary only scratches the surface of the field. One very complex aspect is that heat transfer is a time-dependent function, so the math problems can get complicated. However, the researcher armed with this basic knowledge of heat transfer and how it works will be better prepared to continue the study in advanced physics heat transfer and thermodynamics classes.

Mass

Mass has been described as a measure of the amount of material or stuff that resists a force working on it. We sometimes incorrectly think of weight as equivalent to mass. Weight is really the force of gravity on a given mass. For example, an astronaut may weigh 130 lbs on her home scale, but zero when she is in space visiting the International Space Station. Her mass, however, is the same at home and on the Space Station. Mass does not change based on the forces acting on an object, though weight can change based on the acceleration due to gravity.

Velocity and Acceleration

Sometimes we confuse the terms velocity and acceleration. The difference is that velocity is the instantaneous measure of the change in distance over a change in time. For example, as we drive our car, our speedometer measures our velocity in miles per hour or m/h. Acceleration is the change in velocity over a change in time. So, if we step on the gas, velocity increases; and the rate at which it increases per some measure of time (e.g., second, minute, hour) is acceleration. This shows how they are related measurements, but different.

If x = position or distance, t = time, v = velocity, and a = acceleration, then the following equations apply:

v = change in x/change in time

This is written in shorthand as v = dx/dt.

a = change in v/change in time

This is written in shorthand as a = dv/dt.

These equations show how velocity and acceleration are calculated and how they are related.

Here on Earth we are under the influence of the gravitational pull from the mass of the Earth. This pull is the force of gravity which creates a constant rate of acceleration toward the Earth of 32.2 (feet/sec)/sec or 9.81 (meters/sec)/sec. This is commonly simplified to 32.2 ft/sec² and 9.81 m/sec².

The primary equation that governs force in terms of mass and acceleration is

Force = Mass × Acceleration, abbreviated as an equation F=ma

In the Metric system, the units of measurement are

Force: Newton = N

Mass: Kilograms = kg

Acceleration: Meters per second² = m/s²

In the English system, the units of measurement are

Force: Pounds = lbs

Mass: Slugs or pounds mass = lbm

Acceleration: Feet per second² = ft/s²

"Force is equal to mass times acceleration" is Newton's Second Law of Motion. This is a key equation which establishes how all objects behave and interact. It describes why you stay attached to the Earth; it explains the motions of the planets; it even describes how fast a car or a runner can accelerate.

Is there a good way to show or communicate how force interacts with an object? There is a methodology termed Free Body Diagram which is used to graphically show the location, direction, and magnitude of forces that are being applied to an object (Figure 5-4). These forces can act on an object in different directions. In many cases, a single force is broken down into three components x, y, and z. These vectors are used to analyze how an object moves in these three axes. This is a branch of study termed vector mechanics.

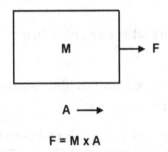

Figure 5-4. *Simple Free Body Diagram of F = M × A*

In the preceding case, there is only one force acting on the object, so it will accelerate to the right. If there were an equal and opposite force acting on the object pulling it to the left, then the sum of all the forces would be zero, and it would not move. If the forces do not sum up to zero, then the object will move in the direction of the greatest force. This is Newton's Third Law of Motion.

Inertia

Inertia is very important; it is stated as once a body is in motion, it stays in motion until acted on by an outside force. This is Newton's First Law of Motion.

Isaac Newton's three Laws of Motion define how many things in the world function and have allowed engineers and scientists to understand and solve many common problems related to moving objects.

Momentum

Momentum describes the potential damage when objects collide and is defined as the product of mass times velocity. The more momentum an object has when it collides with another object, the more damage. So, if a car travels 5 mph and hits something, there may not be much damage. If a car were traveling 65 mph, momentum increases significantly, and the car would certainly cause much greater damage to itself and/or to whatever it hit. A truck, which has more mass than a car, traveling at 65 mph would cause even more damage.

Momentum = mass x velocity, abbreviated as an equation M=mv

Friction

What is friction? When two objects are in contact, and a force exerted on one object causes motion, the object(s) will encounter a resistive force called frictional force. (See Figure 5-5 for a Free Body Diagram showing these forces.) Several factors affect the frictional force: the weight of an object, its surface roughness, the roughness of the surface it rests on, and the force being exerted on it to move it. Other factors that can influence or describe these aspects are the frictional coefficient of the surface and the angle at which an object is being pulled or pushed.

Some key definitions of some of the symbols used in the following equations are as follows:

F_N = The normal force pushing down on the table. The term normal is used because a 90-degree angle is designated a normal angle. It is always perpendicular to the surface an object is sitting on.

F_{Table} = The force of the table pushing or holding the object up.

F_{fr} = This is the frictional force resisting movement of an object. It is a function of the surface and the normal force.

μs and μk = The static (no movement) and dynamic (object in motion) coefficients of friction. They are dependent on the material of the surface finish.

If there is no motion, then the sum of the forces will equal zero (see Figure 5-5):

- Sum of force in Y direction = F_N = F_{Table}.

- F_N= Mass of object × Acceleration due to gravity = mg (g is acceleration due to gravity).

- Sum of force in X direction = F_{fr} = F

- The static coefficient of friction for materials = μs.

- Frictional force that balances the maximum force in X direction prior to motion is F_{fr} = F_N x μs.

The static coefficient friction is in effect when the two objects are not in motion. It is higher than the dynamic coefficient. This is easily seen when a heavy object starts moving, as it takes less force to keep it moving than it took to start the motion.

If there is motion (see Figure 5-5)

- Sum of force in Y direction = F_N = F_{Table} = mg.

- Sum of force in X direction = F_{fr} < F.

- The kinetic coefficient of friction for materials = μk.

- Frictional force that resists the force in X direction causing motion is

$$F_{fr} = FN \times \mu k$$

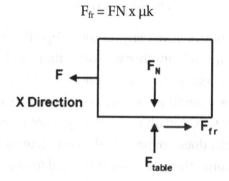

Figure 5-5. *Free Body Diagram Showing Frictional Force*

If F_{fr} is greater than or equal to F, the object will not move. When a car is stopped at a light and is not moving, this is the condition. In the winter, when the roads are icy, the F_{fr} is significantly less. If this car is on a slope, F_{fr} may not be greater than the force F pulling the car down the slope. In this case, the car might start moving, and things get exciting!

The equations for friction may seem complex at first, but keep in mind the Free Body Diagram and how the forces are if there is no motion.

More Advanced Aspects of Calculus

In calculus, there is a mathematical concept which is designated integration. Putting it simply, data is integrated over a variable like time to arrive at a total measurement. It uses the symbol ∫. In the case of an object in motion, the researcher is interested in the change of distance over time and the change of velocity over time. These are interrelated using the following equations.

The standard calculus method of writing integration is

$$x2 - x1 = \int v(t)\, dt$$

where X2 is the final position and X1 is the initial position from t1 to t2. The shorthand way of writing it is velocity $(v) = dx/dt$. This was described at the start of this chapter.

Likewise, for acceleration, the standard calculus method of writing is

$$v2 - v1 = \int a(t)\, dt$$

This shows the change in velocity (or the integration of velocity from t1 to t2). As can be seen, this is another way of writing acceleration: $a = dv/dt$.

One important aspect of the relationship between velocity and acceleration is how acceleration captures and sums up the change in velocity over time. Often an object's velocity is not constant, so an instantaneous velocity does not provide the complete picture of the object's motion. Acceleration over time is needed to describe its motion.

The importance of both integration and the opposite function of taking the derivative allows the scientist or engineer to solve equations for terms of interest and simulate or model the real world.

Summary

This chapter covers a lot of complex concepts at a very high level; however, if something does not make sense, the reader should look over the associated project in this book and other sources online or in other books to gain a better understanding of the complex yet highly useful subjects. A majority of the world behaves based on these simple equations.

CHAPTER 6

Time/Condition-Dependent Projects

This chapter provides details on several projects that are time dependent and condition dependent. What does that mean? For each project, there are two variables measured. In most of these projects, one variable is time. The second variable is the value of interest that the researcher is trying to determine and how it changes over time. This is a key concept in science and engineering because it happens very often and sometimes is very hard to measure. This chapter highlights several very interesting sensors that bring us closer to the *Star Trek* tricorder.

The first two projects demonstrate conduction heat transfer. The third project demonstrates convection heat transfer. The fourth project is an example of simulating zero gravity. The fifth measures friction and examines the difference between a slope and a flat surface. The sixth and final project demonstrates a very nice sensor that can measure acceleration.

These very unique experiments allow the reader to expand their knowledge base in many areas. Additionally, the reader can explore the concepts associated with time-dependent measurement.

Conduction Heat Transfer Through an Aluminum Rod

While we often measure temperature, heat transfer is really an important aspect. Heat transfer is the flow of heat from a hot object to a cold object.

© Paul Bradt and David Bradt 2020
P. Bradt and D. Bradt, *Science and Engineering Projects Using the Arduino and Raspberry Pi*,
https://doi.org/10.1007/978-1-4842-5811-8_6

In this project, we will show a way to measure the heat flowing down an aluminum rod into a cold source. Additionally, from a mathematics perspective, we will show a method to model or simulate the movement of heat through an object.

Science   Develop an understanding of conduction heat transfer.

Technology/Engineering   Using the Arduino and three sensors to measure the flow of heat.

Mathematics   Using real temperature measurements to compare to a simulation of the heat transfer using a parabolic partial differential equation.

This first project demonstrates how heat is transferred along an aluminum rod.

The parts needed are

- Arduino Uno 3

- 3 MCP9700 temperature sensors (see how to add a wire harness in the "Appendix" section)

- Miscellaneous wires and terminal strips

- A bucket of ice water

  - A mixture of ice and water is very close to zero degree C and will maintain that temperature over an extended time period.

- 3/8-inch-diameter, 16-inch-long aluminum rod

  - 12 inches of the rod will be above the ice water, and 4 inches will extend into the ice water.

- Pipe insulation (wrap around the pipe)

- Rod support board

- 1/2-inch foam insulation board

Connect the three temperature sensors per Figures 6-1 and 6-2.

Attach temperature sensors to the aluminum rod using tape at the following positions: 3 inches above the ice bath, 6 inches above the ice bath, and at the end of the rod 12 inches above the ice bath. It is important to tape the sensors so they make good contact with the aluminum rod. One way to ensure this is to file a small flat space on the rod and then tape the sensor there to maximize contact.

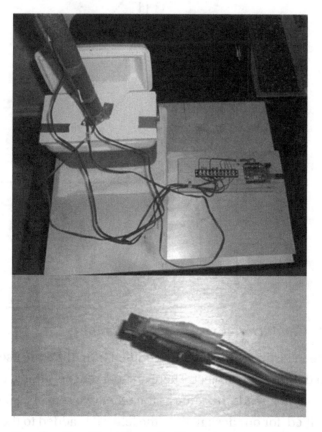

Figure 6-1. *Conduction Heat Transfer Experiment and Sensor Assembly*

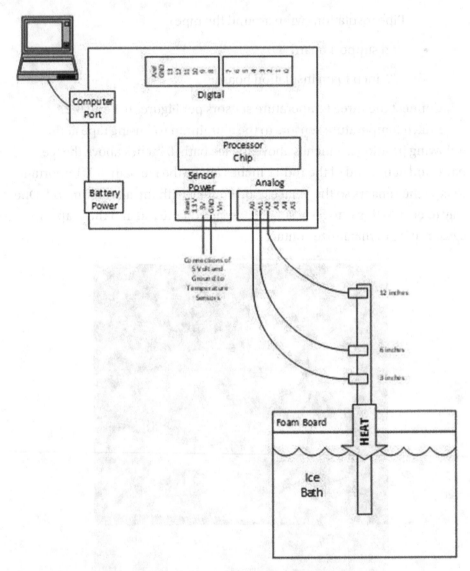

Figure 6-2. *Conduction Experiment Schematic*

The code in Listing 6-1 is slightly modified from the code used in the Arduino data logging project. There are two sensors added, and one is adjusted so that it reads the same as the other two sensors. Since it is slightly modified, for our designation, the letter B is added to the code name to show it is similar but slightly different.

Listing 6-1. Arduino SN102B Three MCP9700 Temperature Sensors
Code

```
//SN102B
//Modified from SN102 with addition three sensors and
//calibration of factor to one sensor
//Original code modified by Paul Bradt from
//Arduino Projects to Save the World
//Published by Apress

int ADC0, ADC1, ADC2;
int MCPoffset = 500;
void setup(){

  Serial.begin(9600);
}
void loop() {

  getADC();
  float temp0 = calcTemp(ADC0, MCPoffset);
  float temp1 = calcTemp(ADC1, MCPoffset)-2;
  float temp2 = calcTemp(ADC2, MCPoffset);
  Serial.print(temp0,0);
  Serial.print(" ");
  Serial.print(temp1,0);
  Serial.print(" ");
  Serial.print(temp2,0);
  Serial.print(" ");
  Serial.println(" ");
  delay(5000);

}
```

```
void getADC() {
  ADC0 = analogRead(A0);
  ADC1 = analogRead(A1);
  ADC2 = analogRead(A2);
}

  float calcTemp (int val,int offset) {
  return((val*4.8828)-offset)/10;

}
```

Ensure Consistency in Temperature Sensor Readings

Before inserting the rod in the ice bath, check the temperature of the three sensors taped to the aluminum rod. If a variance in temperature readings is shown between sensors, a simple sensor calibration will be required. Select the temperature level of one of the sensors that we will call the "base" sensor. Add or subtract the temperature difference (also called the "offset") between the base sensor and each of the other sensors such that all three sensors will read the same temperature. The offset readings are then added or subtracted in the appropriate code as shown in the following to complete the calibration process.

Note in the preceding Arduino code that 2 degrees C is subtracted from the Sensor 1 reading. In the initial comparison between each temperature sensor before the rod was put in the ice bath, Sensor 2 showed a rod temperature offset of 2 degrees higher than the base temperature sensor. Making this change ensures that the temperature sensors are reading consistently and are set for accurate comparisons later in the experiment. Follow the same process if the third sensor has an offset with the base temperature sensor. Determine which sensor is the base temperature sensor by comparing the readings to a digital or mercury thermometer.

Then use that sensor as the base sensor and adjust the other sensors to match it, as demonstrated in the following line of code:

```
float temp1 = calcTemp(ADC1, MCPoffset)-2;
```

Table 6-1 shows some example data gathered for this experiment.

Table 6-1. *Conduction Experiment Data*

	Position and Temp (Degree C)		
Time (min)	3 Inch	6 Inch	12 Inch
0	25	25	25
2	19	24	25
4	19	23	24
6	17	22	23
8	16	21	21
10	15	20	21
12	14	19	20
14	14	19	20
16	14	19	20
18	14	19	19
20	14	18	19

The experiment was run for 20 minutes and is shown in Table 6-1. It is then graphed along with an estimate of the temperature to gain insight. The graph easily shows how temperature changes over time.

For a deeper exploration of this subject, the experimenter can compare the measured results to predictions using the parabolic partial differential equation (PDE). This sounds a lot harder than it is. It is a method that uses previous and surrounding temperatures to predict how a temperature will change over time at specific points. If the reader is interested, see the following information as it uses a simple spreadsheet set up with a PDE that simulates temperature change of the rod as heat is transferred to the ice bath over time.

The equation is from an older textbook source [5] and is added below. It is helpful to understand how each cell interacts from this equation for developing the parabolic partial differential equation in a spreadsheet model.

$$Ti+1,j=Ti,j+K*(Ti,j+1-2*Ti,j+Ti,j-1)$$

where

T = Temperature

i = Time increment

j = Distance increment

K = Factor that includes thermal conductivity, specific heat, density, time increment, and distance increment

Table 6-2 and Figure 6-3 show a spreadsheet and a graph that demonstrates the PDE methodology. In the Excel spreadsheet, time progresses with each row. Each column represents a point on the rod, and the method for calculating a value for a particular cell in this column is to use the cell above to the left, the cell above to the right and the cell directly above to calculate the temperature in the cell being updated (see the preceding equation). To make the spreadsheet work, the boundary cells will need to be set to a number and not a formula. For example, the values at time zero are estimated and are just number values and not calculated.

These values may need to be adjusted to ensure the model makes sense and fits the data reasonably well. The K factor is dependent on several factors. The best way to determine this factor is by testing and checking the value and running the spreadsheet and updating the K value, eventually coming up with the best K that predicts the best match to actual test data points.

When using Excel, one very helpful aid to understand where values go and come from in each cell is to use the Precedents and Dependents tools which are located in the Formulas tab. When you click one of these, arrows show up indicating either the precedent or the dependent cell. Table 6-2 is a screen capture from the spreadsheet that contains the simulation.

Table 6-2. *Parabolic Partial Differential Calculations for Conduction*

	K= Factor that includes, Thermal conductivity, specific heat, density, time increment and distance increment									0.3
	Ice Bath									Ambient Air
Time	Point 0	Point 1	Point 2	Point 3	Point 4	Point 5	Point 6	Point 7	Point 8	Point 9
0	0.00	2.00	16.00	20.00	20.00	20.00	20.00	20.00	20.00	20.00
2	0.00	5.60	13.00	18.80	20.00	20.00	20.00	20.00	20.00	20.00
4	0.00	6.14	12.52	17.42	19.64	20.00	20.00	20.00	20.00	20.00
6	0.00	6.21	12.08	16.62	19.08	19.89	20.00	20.00	20.00	20.00
8	0.00	6.11	11.68	15.99	18.59	19.68	19.97	20.00	20.00	20.00
10	0.00	5.95	11.30	15.48	18.14	19.44	19.89	19.99	20.00	20.00
12	0.00	5.77	10.95	15.02	17.73	19.18	19.79	19.96	20.00	20.00
14	0.00	5.59	10.62	14.61	17.35	18.93	19.66	19.92	19.99	20.00
16	0.00	5.42	10.31	14.24	17.00	18.67	19.52	19.86	19.97	20.00
18	0.00	5.26	10.02	13.89	16.67	18.43	19.37	19.79	19.95	20.00
20	0.00	5.11	9.75	13.56	16.36	18.18	19.21	19.71	19.92	20.00

Figure 6-3 shows the points which are graphed along with a few points from the actual data measured. It can be seen that the actual measured data is very close to the curves from the prediction. Tools like this PDE methodology can be used to determine values when real data cannot be obtained.

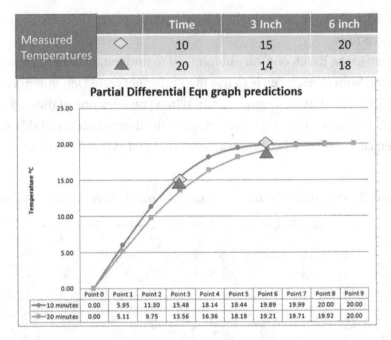

Measured Temperatures		Time	3 Inch	6 inch
	◇	10	15	20
	▲	20	14	18

Partial Differential Eqn graph predictions

	Point 0	Point 1	Point 2	Point 3	Point 4	Point 5	Point 6	Point 7	Point 8	Point 9
10 minutes	0.00	5.95	11.30	15.48	18.14	19.44	19.89	19.99	20.00	20.00
20 minutes	0.00	5.11	9.75	13.56	16.36	18.18	19.21	19.71	19.92	20.00

Figure 6-3. Graph of Partial Differential Equation and Actual Results

Aluminum Rod Conduction Heat Transfer Recap

This project along with the spreadsheet simulation example shows how heat spreads along an object over time. The conduction heat transfer method is utilized extensively in modern computers which have finned heat sinks that pull heat away from the processor chips and keep them cool.

Conduction Heat Transfer Through a Window

This project shows another example of conduction heat transfer. Rather than a long object, the heat flows through a very thin object, a window.

Science   Further develop understanding of conduction heat transfer.

Technology/Engineering   Using the Arduino, two sensors, Real-Time Clock Module, and an SD card data logging shield.

Mathematics   Calculation of heat transfer through a window using a small area to estimate it.

This project uses an LM35 sensor in a sealed TO package. This sealed package along with sealing the small PC board in shrink tubing will help to protect and maintain the effectiveness of this sensor outdoors. This is shown in the Raspberry Pi air buoyancy project in Chapter 4.

The parts needed are

- Arduino Uno (for this project, we must use the Uno to mount the data logging shield to it)

- 2 LM35 temperature sensors and assembled wire harnesses (see section "Raspberry Pi Buoyancy of Air Version" in Chapter 4)

- SparkFun SD card data logging shield product

- SD card

- SparkFun Real-Time Clock Module

- Tape to attach sensors to the window

- Window with access to running wires outside

Connect the hardware per Figures 6-4 and 6-5.

Figure 6-4. *Window Conduction Project*

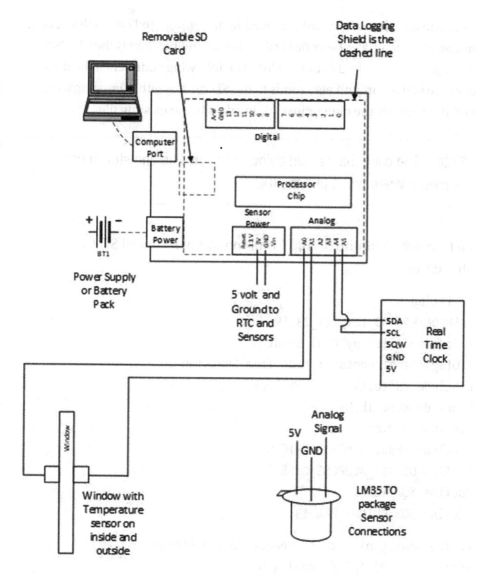

Figure 6-5. *Window Conduction Experiment Schematic*

The code for this project (Listing 6-2) is a combination of two codes for two different SparkFun products. The first product is the Real-Time Clock Module. Once it is set, then it will keep time. This part of the code will need to be run and then afterward will need to be commented out so that it does not reset it each time the code is run. The second product is the SD shield; it plugs into a standard Arduino Uno. The following code sends the data over the serial port and also sends to the SD card by either creating a file and then adding the data or just adding data to the existing file.

Note   The code that is bold below is on one line and should not overwrap when typed into the IDE.

Listing 6-2. Arduino SN106 Combination of RTC and SD Card Shield Code

```
//Listing 6_2
//SN106_RTC_SD_temp_11_23_19
//Code modified by Paul Bradt
//Original elements of code from Sparkfun
#include <Wire.h>
#include <RTClib.h>
#include <SD.h>
#include <SparkFunDS1307RTC.h>
#define DS1307_ADDRESS 0x68
#define SQW_INPUT_PIN 2
#define SQW_OUTPUT_PIN 13

// The analog pins that connect to the sensors
#define tempPin1 0 // analog 0
#define tempPin2 1 // analog 1

const int chipSelect = 8;

float temperature1C = 0.0;
```

```
float temperature2C = 0.0;

String currentDate = "";

RTC_DS1307 RTC;

void setup() {
  Wire.begin();
  Serial.begin(9600);

  Serial.println("SN106 SD and RTC Nov 2019 PDB");

  pinMode(SQW_INPUT_PIN, INPUT_PULLUP);
  pinMode(SQW_OUTPUT_PIN, OUTPUT);
  digitalWrite(SQW_OUTPUT_PIN,
  digitalRead(SQW_INPUT_PIN));

  rtc.begin();
  rtc.writeSQW(SQW_SQUARE_1);

  //This is where time is set:
  //foramt of rtc.setTime(s, m, h, day, date,
  //month, year)where :
  //day = day of the week;date = day of the month
  //The line below will need to be uncommented to
  //set time (put current time in):
  //rtc.setTime(00, 51, 16, 6, 29, 11, 19);
  //After time set then comment it again so does not
  //reset time again.

  Serial.print("Initializing SD card...");
  pinMode(chipSelect, OUTPUT);

  if (!SD.begin(chipSelect)) {
    Serial.println("Card failed, or not present");
    //Exit from program here.
```

```
    return;
  }

  Serial.println("card intialized.");
}

void loop() {
  String updatedDate = printDate();

  File dataFile = SD.open("datalog.txt", FILE_WRITE);

  if (dataFile) {
    dataFile.print(updatedDate);

    Serial.print("Date is: ");
    Serial.print(updatedDate);

    delay(10);
    int tempReading1 = analogRead(tempPin1);
    int tempReading2 = analogRead(tempPin2);

    // converting that reading to temperature C
    temperature1C = (tempReading1 * 4.8828) / 10;
    temperature2C = ((tempReading2 * 4.8828) / 10);

    //write analog sensor data to SD card
    dataFile.print(" Temperature 1");
    dataFile.print(" = ");
    dataFile.print(temperature1C);
    dataFile.print(" Temperature 2");
    dataFile.print(" = ");
    dataFile.print(temperature2C);

    Serial.print(" Temperature 1");
    Serial.print(" = ");
```

```
    Serial.print(temperature1C);
    Serial.print(" Temperature 2");
    Serial.print(" = ");
    Serial.print(temperature2C);

    dataFile.println();

    //create a new row to read data more clearly
    dataFile.close();//close file
    Serial.println();//print to the serial port too:

  }
  else
  {
    Serial.println("error opening datalog.txt");
  }

  delay(5000);
}
String printDate() {
  char tempDate[50];

  rtc.update();
  Wire.beginTransmission(DS1307_ADDRESS);
  byte zero = 0x00;
  Wire.write(zero);
  Wire.endTransmission();
  Wire.requestFrom(DS1307_ADDRESS, 7);

  DateTime currentTime = RTC.now();

  //Print the date like 3/1/1/11 23:59:59
  sprintf(tempDate, "%02d/%02d/%02d %02d:%02d:%02d",
  currentTime.month(), currentTime.day(),
```

```
currentTime.year(), currentTime.hour(),
currentTime.minute(), currentTime.second());
```

```
return String(tempDate);
}
```

When this data was collected and listed in Table 6-3, the temperature outside was cold. The outside and inside temperatures were very low and not significantly different. The data was taken at 5-minute increments for 15 minutes and then averaged as shown in Table 6-3.

Table 6-3. *Window Conduction Experiment Data*

Time of Reading (Minutes)	Temperature Inside (°C)	Temperature Outside (°C)
0	12.98	7.65
5	12.00	7.16
10	11.51	7.16
15	11.51	7.16
Average temperature	12.00	7.28

Analysis of heat transfer:

Use the conduction equation $dq = (k \, dA \, (T_h - T_c))/dx$

where

dq = Heat transfer (Joule/sec)

k = Window conduction heat transfer coefficient = 0.84 Joule/sec-m-C°

dA = Area of window through which heat is transferred = $0.81 \times 1.12 = 0.91 \text{ m}^2$

T_h = Temperature at hot location = 12 °C

T_c = Temperature at cold location = 7.3 °C

dx = Window thickness = 3.2 x 10⁻³ m

dq = ((0.84) * (0.91) * (12 – 7.3))/ 3.2 x 10⁻³ = 1123
Joule/sec

Since 1 Joule/sec = 1 watt, the heat transfer rate through the window is around 1100 watts escaping the house on a cold winter day.

Window Conduction Heat Transfer Recap

This project demonstrates an interesting aspect regarding heat transfer that a high differential temperature on a cold day really drives the high heat transfer rate. It could also be utilized to determine how much heat is driven through a window into a house on a hot day. One more item that can be seen from the equation is that as the temperature changes, the heat transfer rate changes. To get the complete picture and gather data over the day, this setup does not need a computer connected to it. The Arduino will track changes through the day.

Convection Heat Transfer

Convection heat transfer is a somewhat more complex method of heat transfer as it depends on the movement of a gas or fluid passing over a surface. This project utilizes a similar setup to the aluminum rod conduction project, but air is blown across it, and the temperatures at two points on the rod are observed to gather data related to the heat transfer rate and how fast the fan blows.

Science   Develop an understanding of convection heat transfer.

Technology/Engineering   Using the Arduino and two sensors.

Mathematics   Using the temperature conversion and averaging two measurements to calculate the convection heat transfer.

The parts needed are

- Arduino Uno 3

- 2 MCP9700 temperature sensors (assembled with wire harness)

- Miscellaneous wires and terminal strips

- A bucket of ice water

  - A mixture of ice and water is very close to zero degree C and will maintain that temperature over an extended time period.

- 3/8-inch-diameter, 16-inch-long aluminum rod

  - 12 inches of the rod will be above the ice water, and 4 inches will extend into the ice water.

- Rod support board

- 1/2-inch foam insulation board

Build up the system per Figures 6-6 and 6-7.

Figure 6-6. *Convection Experiment*

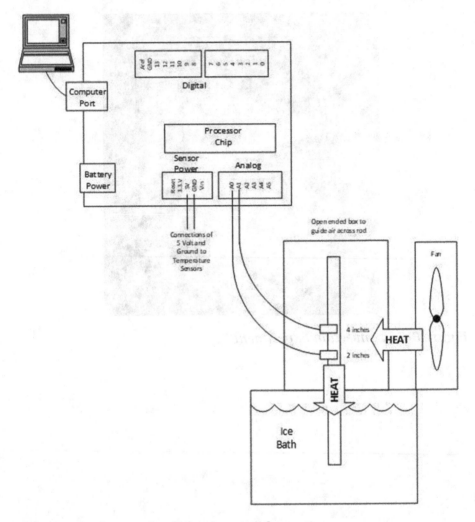

Figure 6-7. *Convection Experiment Schematic*

The code in Listing 6-3 is basically the same as that used in the first conduction project with the exception of only two sensors, not three.

Listing 6-3. Arduino SN102B Two MCP9700 Temperature Sensors
Code

```
//SN102B
//Modified from SN102 with addition two sensors and
//calibration of factor to one sensor
//Original code modified from Arduino Projects to
//Save the World
//Published by Apress
int ADC0, ADC1;
int MCPoffset = 500;

void setup(){
  Serial.begin(9600);
}

void loop() {
  getADC();
  float temp0 = calcTemp(ADC0, MCPoffset);
  float temp1 = calcTemp(ADC1, MCPoffset)-2;
  Serial.print(temp0,0);
  Serial.print(" ");
  Serial.print(temp1,0);
  Serial.print(" ");
  Serial.println(" ");
  delay(10000);
}

void getADC() {
  ADC0 = analogRead(A0);
  ADC1 = analogRead(A1);
}
```

```
float calcTemp (int val,int offset) {
  return((val*4.8828)-offset)/10;
}
```

The data collected using this system is shown in Table 6-4.

Table 6-4. *Data from the Convection Experiment*

Fan Speed	2 Inches	4 Inches	Average Temperature	Ambient Temperature	Delta in Temperature
Off	18	20	19	24	5
Low	20	21	20.5	24	3.5
High	20	22	21	24	3

Convection Heat Transfer Recap

The preceding data shows how a higher flow rate of air across the rod increases the heat transfer and causes the temperature to become more uniform. This experiment demonstrates convection heat transfer; and we use it often, for example, when we try to cool off a hot spoon of soup by blowing on it before we eat it.

Zero Gravity Demonstration

What precisely is zero gravity? When we stand on the Earth, its gravitational force pulls us down, and we stay in contact with the ground. To achieve zero gravity, the forces must either balance out, or the object must be far enough away that the force of attraction between the two objects is very low. Figure 6-8 and the following equation show how the gravitational attraction works on an object in motion upward from the Earth.

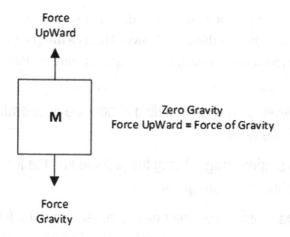

Figure 6-8. Zero Gravity Free Body Diagram

$$F = (G \times M \times m)/r^2$$

where

F = Force of gravity between the objects. Unit is N.

G = Gravitational constant and in SI units = 6.674×10^{-11} N·m²·kg⁻².

M = Larger mass units are Kg.

m = Smaller mass units are Kg.

r = Distance between the centers of the objects in meters.

As can be seen from the equation, a very massive object, like the Earth, dominates the force of attraction between the two objects. Also if the objects are close, then the force of attraction will be significantly higher. For example, the reader could calculate the gravitational force on them at the surface of the Earth and then compare that to the force at the International Space Station which is approximately 400 kilometers above the Earth's surface. Don't forget to include the actual distance from the center of the Earth in the calculations!

The system in this project monitors the change of the force exerted on an object as it flies up and then falls down. This is a unique project because it will demonstrate a way to simulate zero gravity here on Earth.

Science   Develop an understanding of how the acceleration due to gravity and force work.

Technology/Engineering   Using the Arduino and the force sensor to measure simulated zero gravity.

Mathematics   Using the direct measurement from the force sensor to develop a graph showing the force of gravity while an object goes from rest to the top of its trajectory where forces are balanced by the upward thrust resulting in zero force on the sensor. Also using curve smoothing in Excel.

The parts needed are

- Arduino Uno 3

- Round force sensor

- 10K Ω resistor

- Miscellaneous wires, proto-board, and terminal strips

The parts needed to change a compression sensor into a tension sensor (see Figures 6-9 to 6-12) are

- 2 U-bolts and 6 nuts

- 1 square piece of wood with four holes matching the U-bolts

- Flat metal plate with two holes which match the U-bolts

- Adhesive rubber bumper attached to the flat plate which pushes on the sensor

Assemble the system that converts the force sensor to a tension sensor as shown in Figures 6-9 through 6-12. This configuration is similar to a device called a tension load cell. With the sensor hanging from the top U-bolt, when force is applied to the bottom U-bolt, the sensor senses that force.

How does this device work? The upper U-bolt provides a means of holding the sensor up. The lower U-bolt pulls down on the plate with its own weight. This force is transmitted to the force sensor because the rubber bumper is resting on it. Four nuts are only on the upper U-bolt and clamp it to the board. The other two nuts are on the lower U-bolt and ensure it will not slip through the flat metal plate.

(The sensor is attached to the wood with double-sided tape.)

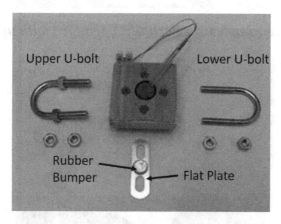

Figure 6-9. *Components for Tension Sensor*

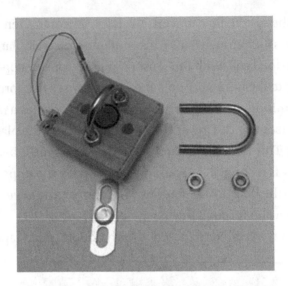

Figure 6-10. *Tension Sensor Partially Assembled with upper U-Bolt*

Figure 6-11. *Fully Assembled Tension Sensor with lower U-Bolt and Plate Which Pushes on It*

Build the test support structure (see Figures 6-12 through 6-14). This setup consists of a base, an upright support that supports the drawer slide, and a block attached to one of the tabs that was connected to the drawer. This block has a hook on it, and the tension sensor hangs from this hook. The drawer slide ensures the force sensor assembly travels up and down on a controlled path. This can be seen in Figure 6-14. The weight of the lower U-bolt will push down on the force sensor as it goes up. Then as the force sensor travels down, the lower U-bolt will lift off the force sensor, and at the top there will be no force simulating zero gravity.

Connect the sensor and resistor to the Arduino.

Set up the slide-up and test that it moves freely and records data.

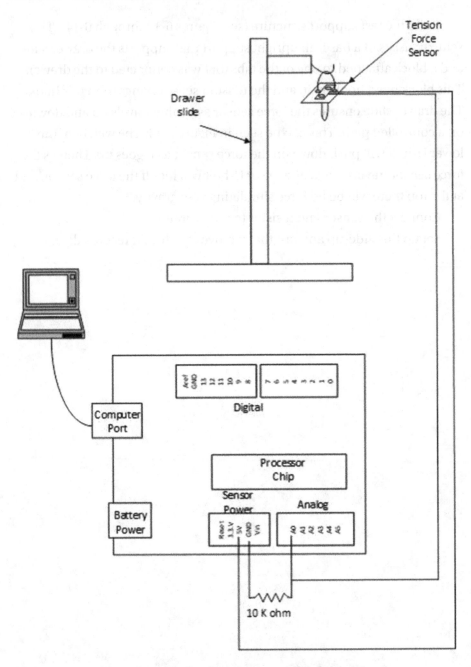

Figure 6-12. *Zero Gravity Project Setup and Schematic*

The same code (Listing 4-3 or 4-4) used in the previous force/pressure project (Code SN104 or SN104B) is used for this project. For this experiment, the scientist will need to modify either code by speeding up the data collection. To do this in the SN104 code, uncomment the delay (100) line and comment the delay (5000) line. Uncommenting the code implements the shorter delay time. Commenting the code by adding // in front of the line causes the Arduino to ignore that line of code.

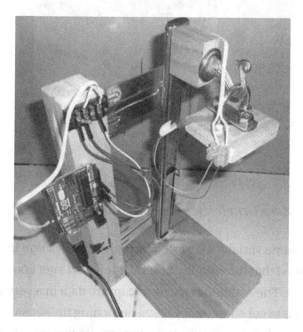

Figure 6-13. *Zero Gravity Sensor at the Bottom*

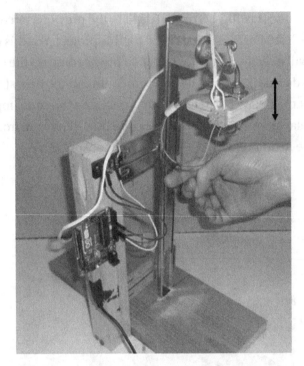

Figure 6-14. *Zero Gravity Sensor Being Tossed Up in the Air*

There are some variables (Exerted force upward, friction in the drawer slide, and others) that may require several attempts to get good data on this experiment. The Arduino is trying to capture data in a very short time, and it is difficult to get consistency when launching the sensor assembly using the drawer slide to guide its trajectory straight up into the air. The experimenter should try several attempts and use the best results they obtain. The data is collected (an example set collected is listed in Table 6-5) and then graphed as shown in Figure 6-15.

Table 6-5. *Example Data from the Zero Gravity Force Experiment*

Force	296	479	195	0	0	0	0	40	359	225	159
Msec	0	100	200	300	400	500	600	700	800	900	1000

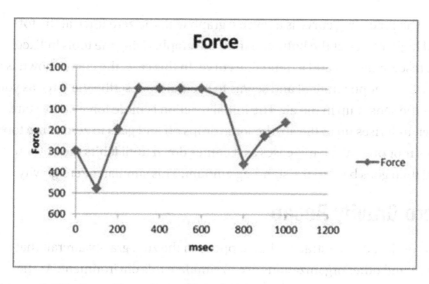

Figure 6-15. *Raw Force Data Graph*

The preceding graph is a reverse graph with the higher force measurement at the bottom. The points are connected, but in reality it would not be disjointed or flat as this seems to indicate.

Figure 6-16 is the same data but smoothed out using Excel tools.

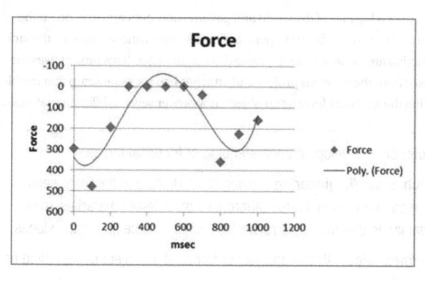

Figure 6-16. *Force Data Graph with Smoothing*

117

The preceding curve is a reverse graph with the zero force at the top and higher force at the bottom part of the graph. Using the tools in Excel, the researcher can add a trend line curve. In this case, the curve shown is a fourth-order polynomial and seems to accurately describe the force as you toss the sensor up in the air. The initial reaction is more force at the start. Then as it rises up in the air, the force drops off and goes to zero at the top of its motion. Then it increases as it comes down until it hits the bottom and then goes back to the standing amount. This simulates zero gravity.

Zero Gravity Recap

This project demonstrates what happens in the zero gravity aircraft that NASA and other organizations use to simulate this environment. As the aircraft goes up over the top of its flight path, there are a few moments where the upward force on the object balances the downward pull gravity. For this brief time, it simulates zero gravity.

Measuring Frictional Force Projects

Friction is a big part of the world and governs how our cars drive down the road and how we walk on slippery surfaces. Friction and sometimes the lack of friction are evident when trying to drive a car on ice. This project uses the sensor from the previous project and attaches it to a special setup that enables testing the frictional force as an object moves over several different materials.

Science   Develop an understanding of frictional forces.

Technology/Engineering   Using the Arduino and the force sensor to measure frictional force differences on different materials. Also evaluating the difference related to frictional force on angled slopes.

Mathematics   Vector analysis of forces of an object being pulled up an incline.

Arduino Frictional Force Project

The parts needed are

- Arduino Uno 3

- Round force sensor

- 10K ohm resistor

- Tension sensor from the previous project

- Miscellaneous boards, pulleys, fasteners to set up slope friction test rig

This project uses the force sensor and a device that converts it from a compression-measuring device into a tension-measuring device, and the instructions on how to build it are shown in the previous zero gravity project.

Adafruit has a very good description of how this sensor works along with a calibration curve showing where it is linear and where it is not. The "Appendix" section at the back of this book shows the technique needed to solder the wires to the round force sensor. When it is connected to the Arduino, the resistor is part of a voltage divider and is compared to the normal resistor.

The slope test apparatus for this experiment consists of two main sections which are attached together as shown in Figures 6-17 and 6-18. The first section consists of the base of the apparatus and the piece that has the test surfaces attached to it. The test surface section is attached to the base with a hinge to allow it to pivot to different angles. To set the angles of this inclined plane from 15 degrees and 30 degrees, two more small pieces of support wood were cut at those angles. These were attached with angle brackets to the base piece and with a screw to the test surface piece (inclined plane). A pulley was attached to the test section piece to direct the string up to the tension sensor. The second section is the upright support, and it holds the tension sensor above the slope and keeps it high enough for the steepest test angle. The last part needed is the test block that is pulled along the test surface and is a wood block, but another material could be substituted.

For this experiment, there were three test surfaces utilized. The first was a thin piece of styrene plastic (which can be found at a hobby shop or online). The second was the plain test surface which was wood. The final test surface was fine-grade sandpaper. Even fine-grade sandpaper caused the block to catch and jerk loose. Rough-grade sandpaper might make it difficult to gather good data.

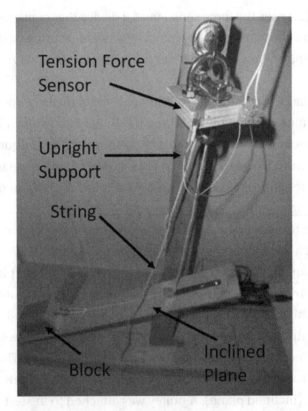

Figure 6-17. *Frictional Force Experiment*

Operational Schematic

The same code (Listing 4-3 or 4-4) used in the previous force/pressure project (Code SN104 or SN104B) is used for this project.

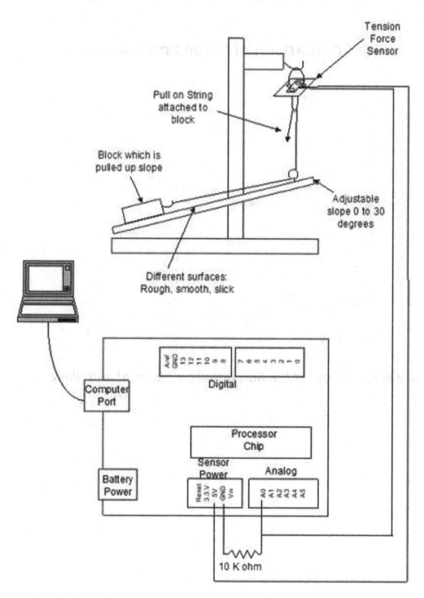

Figure 6-18. *Frictional Force Setup and Schematic*

The data shown in Figure 6-19 is an average of a few readings. The increasing force makes sense due to the increased slope, but is this increase caused by more friction or because the object is being lifted as it goes up the slope? Let's analyze it using a Free Body Diagram in Figure 6-20.

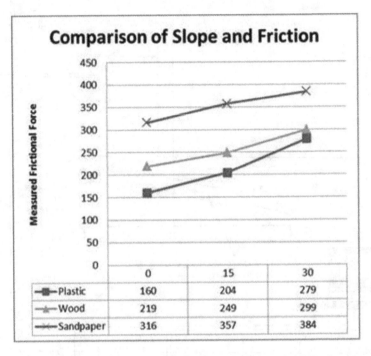

Comparison of Slope and Friction			
	0	15	30
Plastic	160	204	279
Wood	219	249	299
Sandpaper	316	357	384

Figure 6-19. *Graph of Friction Based on Material and Slope*

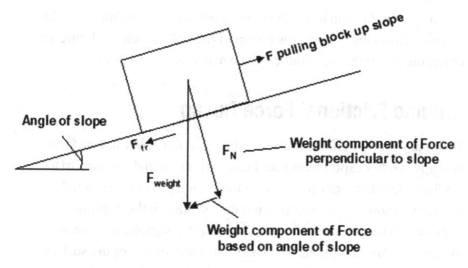

Figure 6-20. *Free Body Diagram Showing Forces on the Object Being Pulled Up the Slope*

Friction equation: $F_{Fr} = F_N \times \mu s$

Also, of note, the sensor is actually seeing twice the force that is exerted on the block of wood. (See Figure 6-21.)

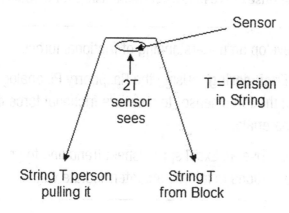

Figure 6-21. *Free Body Diagram Showing Forces on the Sensor*

Analyzing the data in greater detail along with the inclined Free Body diagram shows that the increasing force is actually a factor of lifting the object higher up the slope rather than an increase in friction.

Arduino Frictional Force Recap

This setup allows a good comparison between materials and surfaces. Perhaps another experiment could compare a material and/or surface configuration that really resists movement. Or try to find a material that resists more in one direction but not as much in the opposite or perpendicular direction (such as wood with a significant grain or roughness). Another potential area to test would be wet or dry surfaces. Another possible area for investigation is the friction on ice.

Raspberry Pi Frictional Force Project

This project provides another way to measure friction force and then track the data on the Raspberry Pi. The authors also analyzed the nonlinear force sensor response curve in greater detail using some tools in Excel.

Science   Develop an understanding of frictional forces.

Technology/Engineering   Using the Raspberry Pi, analog to digital converter, and the force sensor to measure frictional force differences on different materials.

Mathematics   Use an Excel spreadsheet trend line to graph data and use the equations to interpolate intermediate values.

The parts needed are

- Raspberry Pi 3

- MCM 40-pin GPIO breakout board and cable for Raspberry Pi (or equivalent)

- Small round force sensor

- MCP3008 analog to digital converter

- Miscellaneous wires, proto-board, and terminal strips

- 10K Ω resistor

This project uses the same friction measure system and supporting device from the previous project; see Figures 6-22 and 6-23. It has a stand and the device that changes the force sensor from a compression-measuring device into a tension-measuring device. This tension sensor device construction is shown in the zero gravity project (Figures 6-9, 6-10, and 6-11), and it was also used in the Arduino friction project.

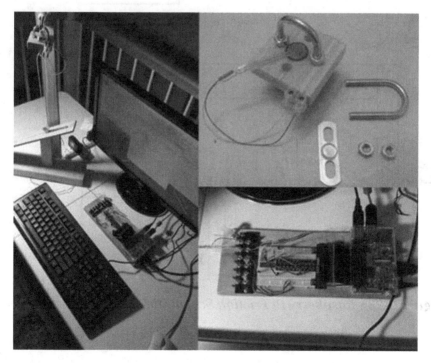

Figure 6-22. *Raspberry Pi Friction Experiment*

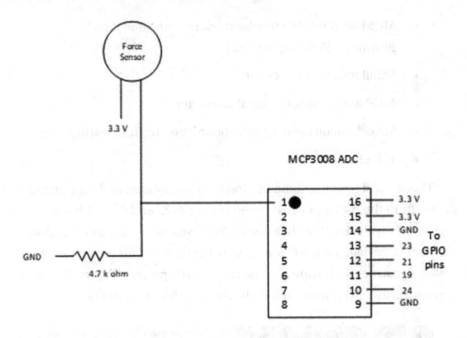

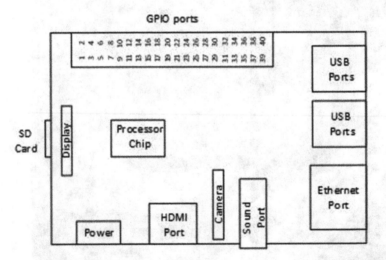

Figure 6-23. *Raspberry Pi Friction Schematic*

The code for this project (Listing 6-4) is similar to the buoyancy code (Listing 4-2) but only uses one sensor input. It also converts the reading to percentage of full scale. This allows the reader to take this percentage and calculate a reading based on the graph developed in the analysis section of this topic.

Note   The following four lines of Bold code below are on one line in the program.

Listing 6-4. Raspberry Pi Code PI_SN002B One Analog Force Sensor

```
# Pi_SN002B is a Modification by Paul Bradt
# Simple example of reading the MCP3008 analog input # channels
# Convert to Force
# Original code from Author: Tony DiCola
# License: Public Domain

import time

# Import SPI library (for hardware SPI) and MCP3008 library.
import Adafruit_GPIO.SPI as SPI
import Adafruit_MCP3008

# Software SPI configuration:
CLK  = 23
CS   = 24
MISO = 21
MOSI = 19
mcp = Adafruit_MCP3008.MCP3008(clk=CLK, cs=CS, miso=MISO, mosi=MOSI)
```

```
# Hardware SPI configuration:
# SPI_PORT   = 0
# SPI_DEVICE = 0
# mcp = Adafruit_MCP3008.MCP3008(spi=SPI.SpiDev(SPI_PORT, SPI_DEVICE))
print('Reading MCP3008 digital values from Force Sensor')

# Main program loop.
while True:
    # Read all the ADC channel values in a list.
    values = [0]*8
    for i in range(8):
    # The read_adc function will get the value for two channels (0-1).
        values[i] = mcp.read_adc(i)
    #Math for converting raw digital value to percentage full
    scale of sensor
    values[1] = values[0]/1023.0*100.0
    print('| {0:>4} Raw| {1:>4} %| '.format(*values))
    # Pause for half a second.
    time.sleep(0.5)
```

The following Adafruit web site below has a lot of good information regarding this force sensor. The graph on this site seems to show that response (resistance to force) looks linear, but it is in reality a log–log graph. The standard linear interpolation calculation will not work as this is a nonlinear relationship. However, the graph and analysis later in the chapter can be utilized. With a measured resistance and the analysis, a better estimate of the force is the result.

www.adafruit.com/product/166

The graph in Figure 6-24 utilizes spreadsheet tools and the information regarding the force sensor to create trend line equations in Excel to develop a way to estimate the force given a resistance reading across the sensor. The authors created this graph by putting in two endpoints where the force sensor responded in linear fashion on a log–log scale per the Adafruit site. These points are 16 grams at 10 ohms and 1000 grams at 1.5 ohms. This is a negative sloped relationship. Per the force sensor data sheet, it is a power–law relationship. To simulate this, the authors using Excel compared a linear trend line, log trend line, and power trend line and then used the trend line equations to calculate endpoints and an intermediate force value at 6 ohms. The power trend line really shows a very nonlinear response. The force value changes significantly given a very small resistance change, in particular, at the high force range. This type of calculation can be used to fine-tune the sensor or refine the prediction of force value based on the change in resistance.

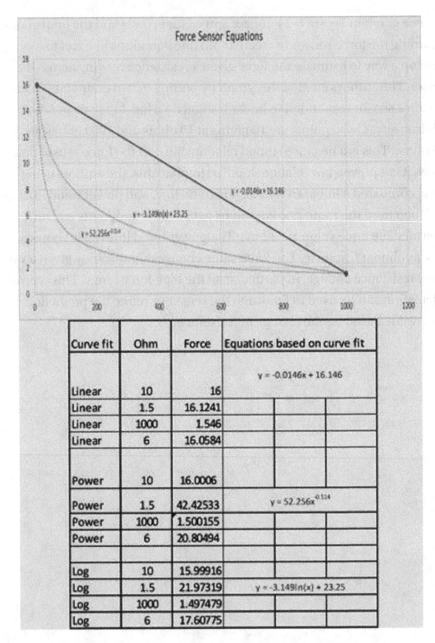

Figure 6-24. *Graph of Force Sensor Data and Calculations*

Raspberry Pi Frictional Force Recap

This project expands on the frictional force experiment by using a Raspberry Pi and ADC along with a spreadsheet to develop a nonlinear equation to estimate values quickly when reading the percentage of full scale.

Acceleration Projects

As described in Chapter 5, the acceleration of an object is an important concept. In this section, the first project measures the acceleration of a baseball bat. The second project measures the acceleration of a car or objects inside and can provide very useful data. An example use of this type of project is when automobile companies crash their cars and use test dummies to see how devices like airbags protect humans from the rapid deceleration and hitting objects.

Acceleration Direct to Computer

This project uses an amazing sensor, the ADXL345 sensor, that captures the acceleration in the x, y, and z axes. This project uses it to measure the acceleration of a bat as it is swung. Remember **safety first** when swinging a bat. Make sure no one is in the area.

Science   Measure the acceleration of an object as it speeds up and slows down.

Technology/Engineering   Using the Arduino and a very unique sensor that measures the acceleration in the x, y, and z axes.

Mathematics   Vector analysis of the acceleration of an object.

The parts needed are

- Arduino Uno

- Computer

- ADXL 345 acceleration sensor (SparkFun)

- Baseball bat

- Extra-long USB extension cable

- Miscellaneous hardware (wire, prototype board, wood, and zip ties)

The setup is put together as shown in Figures 6-25 and 6-26.

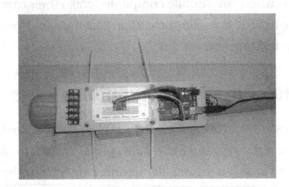

Figure 6-25. *Swinging a Bat Acceleration Project*

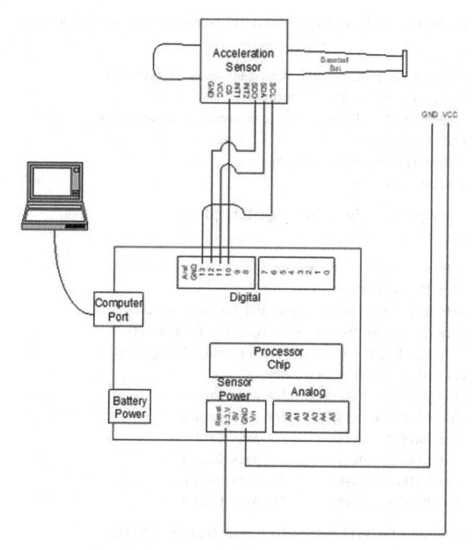

Figure 6-26. *Swinging a Bat Project Schematic*

The code in Listing 6-5 is modified slightly from the SparkFun web site. The SPI library will need to be obtained to get it to operate.

Note   The code that is bold below is on one line and should not overwrap when typed into the IDE.

Listing 6-5. Arduino SN107_ADXL345 Acceleration Sensor to Computer

```
//SN107
//This code captures the data and sends it over the
//serial port to the computer
//Add the SPI library so we can communicate with the
//ADXL345 sensor
//Code from Sparkfun website
#include <SPI.h>

//Assign the Chip Select signal to pin 10.
int CS=10;

//This is a list of some of the registers available
//on the ADXL345.
//To learn more about these and the rest of the
//registers on the ADXL345, read the datasheet!
char POWER_CTL = 0x2D;    //Power Control Register
char DATA_FORMAT = 0x31;
char DATAX0 = 0x32;       //X-Axis Data 0
char DATAX1 = 0x33;       //X-Axis Data 1
char DATAY0 = 0x34;       //Y-Axis Data 0
char DATAY1 = 0x35;       //Y-Axis Data 1
char DATAZ0 = 0x36;       //Z-Axis Data 0
char DATAZ1 = 0x37;       //Z-Axis Data 1

//This buffer will hold values read from the ADXL345
//registers.
char values[10];
//These variables will be used to hold the x,y and z axis
accelerometer values.
int x,y,z;
```

```
void setup(){
  //Initiate an SPI communication instance.
  SPI.begin();

  //Configure the SPI connection for the ADXL345.
  SPI.setDataMode(SPI_MODE3);

  //Create a serial connection to display the data on
  //the terminal.
  Serial.begin(9600);

  //Set up the Chip Select pin to be an output from
  //the Arduino.
  pinMode(CS, OUTPUT);

  //Before communication starts, the Chip Select pin
  //needs to be set high.
  digitalWrite(CS, HIGH);

  //Put the ADXL345 into +/- 4G range by writing the
  //value 0x01 to the DATA_FORMAT register.
  writeRegister(DATA_FORMAT, 0x01);

  //Put the ADXL345 into Measurement Mode by writing
  //0x08 to the POWER_CTL register.
  writeRegister(POWER_CTL, 0x08);
  //Measurement mode
}

void loop(){
  //Reading 6 bytes of data starting at register
  //DATAX0 will retrieve the x,y and z acceleration
  //values from the ADXL345.
  //The results of the read operation will get stored
  //to the values[] buffer.
  readRegister(DATAX0, 6, values);
```

```
//The ADXL345 gives 10-bit acceleration values, but
//they are stored as bytes (8-bits). To get the
//full value, two bytes must be combined for each
//axis.
//The X value is stored in values[0] and values[1].
x = ((int)values[1]<<8)|(int)values[0];

//The Y value is stored in values[2] and values[3].
y = ((int)values[3]<<8)|(int)values[2];

//The Z value is stored in values[4] and values[5].
z = ((int)values[5]<<8)|(int)values[4];

//Print the results to the terminal.
Serial.print(x, DEC);
Serial.print(',');
Serial.print(y, DEC);
Serial.print(',');
Serial.println(z, DEC);
  delay(500);
}

//This function will write a value to a register on
//the ADXL345 Parameters:
//char registerAddress - The register to write a
//value to
//char value - The value to be written to the
//specified register.
void writeRegister(char registerAddress, char value){
  //Set Chip Select pin low to signal the beginning
  //of an SPI packet.
  digitalWrite(CS, LOW);

  //Transfer the register address over SPI.
  SPI.transfer(registerAddress);
```

```
  //Transfer the desired register value over SPI.
    SPI.transfer(value);

  //Set the Chip Select pin high to signal the end of
  //an SPI packet.
    digitalWrite(CS, HIGH);
}
```

```
//This function will read a certain number of
//registers starting from a specified address and
//store their values in a buffer.
//Parameters:
//  char registerAddress - The register address to
//start the read sequence from.
//  int numBytes - The number of registers that
//should be read.
//  char * values - A pointer to a buffer where the
//results of the operation should be stored.
```

```
void readRegister(char registerAddress, int numBytes, char * values){
  //Since we're performing a read operation, the most
  //significant bit of the register address should
  //be set.
  char address = 0x80 | registerAddress;

  //If we're doing a multi-byte read, bit 6 needs to
  //be set as well.
  if(numBytes > 1)address = address | 0x40;

  //Set the Chip select pin low to start an SPI
  //packet.
  digitalWrite(CS, LOW);

  //Transfer the starting register address that needs
```

```
//to be read.
SPI.transfer(address);

//Continue to read registers until we've read the
//number specified, storing the results to the
// input buffer.
for(int i=0; i<numBytes; i++){
  values[i] = SPI.transfer(0x00);
}

//Set the Chips Select pin high to end the SPI
//packet.
digitalWrite(CS, HIGH);
}
```

Copy and paste the data into a spreadsheet. Several tests were needed, before consistent data was obtained. An example is shown in Table 6-6.

Table 6-6. *Data from the Acceleration of Bat Experiment*

Data pt	1	2	3	4	5	6	7	8
Msec	0	100	200	300	400	500	600	700
G Level	0.28	1.15	3.20	4.00	4.11	4.08	1.09	0.28

The data from the sensor was converted to g level based on the range of the sensor. The conversion factor from the SparkFun web site is 0.0078. The total g level was calculated by combining the acceleration of all three components mathematically using the Pythagorean Theorem as expanded to three dimensions. Pythagoras determined that for a right triangle, the hypotenuse is the square root of the square of the x and y legs of the triangle.

The total vector for acceleration $A = (x^2 + y^2 + z^2)^{0.5}$ or the square root of the sum of the squares.

This data was then captured on the graph in Figure 6-27.

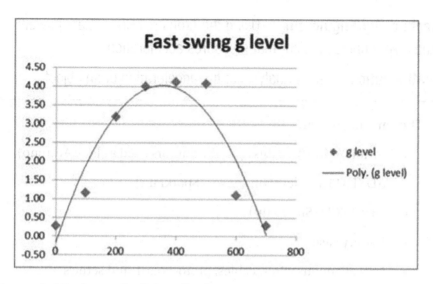

Figure 6-27. *Smoothed Graph of Bat Swing Acceleration*

Acceleration with Computer Recap

The data in Figure 6-27 shows how the acceleration ramps up, quickly peaks, and then drops off fast as the batter reaches the end of the swing. The trend line applied is a second-order polynomial and reflects a smoother transition of the acceleration change.

Acceleration Measurement Without a Computer

This project uses the ADXL345 sensor connected to an Arduino with an LCD and a battery supply to measure the acceleration of a car. Remember **safety first**. Make sure the driver is focused on driving and the passenger is reading the acceleration. Also the reader might want to use an empty parking lot to ensure there are no other vehicles around during the test.

Science   This project utilizes the accelerometer sensor to develop a system to gain insight into how fast an object speeds up and then can slow down.

Technology/Engineering   Using the Arduino, LCD, battery power, and a very unique sensor that measures acceleration.

Mathematics   Vector analysis of the acceleration of an object.

The parts needed are

- Arduino Uno 3 (in this case, the authors used a clone Arduino)

- ADXL345 acceleration sensor (SparkFun)

- 16 × 2 LCD (SparkFun)

- Battery case

- Miscellaneous wires, cables, proto-board, and screws and double-sided tape to hold the battery case

This project integrates the Arduino, LCD, battery pack, and AXDL 345 acceleration sensor in a nice package to use in a car as it speeds up and slows down. See Figures 6-28 and 6-29.

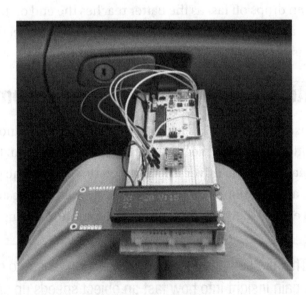

Figure 6-28. *Acceleration Project with LCD*

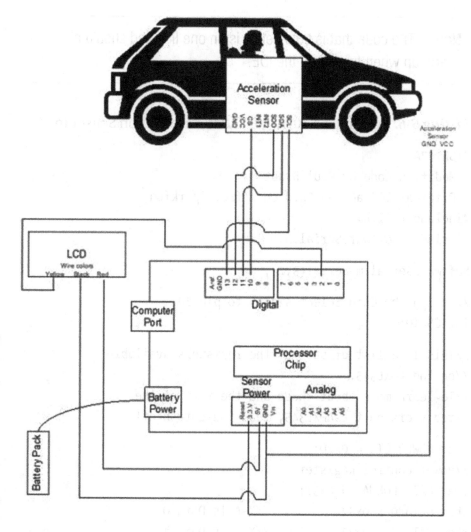

Figure 6-29. *Acceleration Project with LCD Schematic*

The following code (Listing 6-6) is modified from two sets of code on the SparkFun web site. One piece of code is for the accelerometer, and the second code is for the LCD. It captures the acceleration and sends it over the serial port to the Arduino which displays it on the LCD.

This project needs to have the SPI.h and SoftwareSerial.h libraries loaded.

Note   The code that is bold below is on one line and should not overwrap when typed into the IDE.

Listing 6-6. Arduino SN107A_ADXL345 Acceleration Sensor to LCD

```
//SN107A
//Modified Code by Paul Bradt
//Original LCD and SD Card code from Sparkfun
#include <SPI.h>
#include <SoftwareSerial.h>

SoftwareSerial mySerial(3,2);

//Assign the Chip Select signal to pin 10.
int CS=10;

//This is a list of some of the registers available
//on the ADXL345.
//To learn more about these and the rest of the
//registers on the ADXL345, read the datasheet!

char POWER_CTL = 0x2D;
//Power Control Register
char DATA_FORMAT = 0x31;
char DATAX0 = 0x32;         //X-Axis Data 0
char DATAX1 = 0x33;         //X-Axis Data 1
char DATAY0 = 0x34;         //Y-Axis Data 0
char DATAY1 = 0x35;         //Y-Axis Data 1
char DATAZ0 = 0x36;         //Z-Axis Data 0
char DATAZ1 = 0x37;         //Z-Axis Data 1

//This buffer will hold values read from the ADXL345
//registers.
char values[10];
```

142

```
//These variables will be used to hold the x,y and z
//axis accelerometer values.
int x,y,z;

void setup(){
  //Initiate an SPI communication instance.
  SPI.begin();

  //Configure the SPI connection for the ADXL345.
  SPI.setDataMode(SPI_MODE3);

  //Create a serial connection to display the data on
  //the terminal.
  Serial.begin(9600);
  mySerial.begin(9600);

  //Set up the Chip Select pin to be an output from
  //the Arduino.
  pinMode(CS, OUTPUT);

  //Before communication starts, the Chip Select pin
  //needs to be set high.
  digitalWrite(CS, HIGH);

  //Put the ADXL345 into +/- 4G range by writing the
  //value 0x01 to the DATA_FORMAT register.
  writeRegister(DATA_FORMAT, 0x01);

  //Put the ADXL345 into Measurement Mode by writing
  //0x08 to the POWER_CTL register.
  writeRegister(POWER_CTL, 0x08);
  //Measurement mode
}
```

```
void loop(){
  //Reading 6 bytes of data starting at register
  //DATAX0 will retrieve the x,y
  //and z acceleration values from the ADXL345.
  //The results of the read operation will get stored
  //to the values[] buffer.
  readRegister(DATAX0, 6, values);

  //The ADXL345 gives 10-bit acceleration values, but
  //they are stored as bytes
  //(8-bits). To get the full value, two bytes must
  //be combined for each axis.
  //The X value is stored in values[0] and values[1].
  x = ((int)values[1]<<8)|(int)values[0];

  //The Y value is stored in values[2] and values[3].
  y = ((int)values[3]<<8)|(int)values[2];

  //The Z value is stored in values[4] and values[5].
  z = ((int)values[5]<<8)|(int)values[4];

  //Print the results to the terminal.
  Serial.print(x, DEC);
  Serial.print(',');
  Serial.print(y, DEC);
  Serial.print(',');
  Serial.println(z, DEC);

  //Clear the Sparkfun screen LCD first
  mySerial.write(254);
  //move cursor to beginning of first line
  mySerial.write(128);

  mySerial.write("                    ");
```

```
  // clear display
  mySerial.write("                    ");

  mySerial.write(254);
  mySerial.write(128);

  //Print to Sparkfun LCD screen here

  mySerial.print("X: ");
  mySerial.print(x);
  mySerial.print(" Y:");
  mySerial.print(y);

  //Move cursor to second row on LCD

  mySerial.write(254);
  mySerial.write(192);

  mySerial.print("Z: ");
  mySerial.print(z);

  delay(500);
}

//This function will write a value to a register on
// the ADXL345.
//Parameters:
//  char registerAddress - The register to write a
//value to
//  char value - The value to be written to the
// specified register.
void writeRegister(char registerAddress, char value){
  //Set Chip Select pin low to signal the beginning
  //of an SPI packet.
  digitalWrite(CS, LOW);
```

```
  //Transfer the register address over SPI.
  SPI.transfer(registerAddress);

  //Transfer the desired register value over SPI.
    SPI.transfer(value);

  //Set the Chip Select pin high to signal the end of
  //an SPI packet.
  digitalWrite(CS, HIGH);
}

//This function will read a certain number of
//registers starting from a specified
//address and store their values in a buffer.
//Parameters:
//  char registerAddress - The register address to
// start the read sequence from.
//  int numBytes - The number of registers that
//should be read.
//  char * values - A pointer to a buffer where the
// results of the operation should
//be stored.
void readRegister(char registerAddress, int numBytes, char * values){
  //Since we're performing a read operation, the most
  //significant bit of the register address should be
  //set.
  char address = 0x80 | registerAddress;

  //If we're doing a multi-byte read, bit 6 needs to
  //be set as well.
  if(numBytes > 1)address = address | 0x40;
```

```
//Set the Chip select pin low to start an SPI
//packet.
digitalWrite(CS, LOW);

//Transfer the starting register address that needs
//to be read.
SPI.transfer(address);

//Continue to read registers until we've read the
//number specified, storing
//the results to the input buffer.
for(int i=0; i<numBytes; i++){
  values[i] = SPI.transfer(0x00);
}
//Set the Chips Select pin high to end the SPI
//packet.
digitalWrite(CS, HIGH);
}
```

A few experiments were run and some data gathered as shown in Table 6-7.

Table 6-7. *Data from the Automobile Acceleration Experiment*

Msec	0	100	200	300	400
G Level	0.6318	0.7956	0.9633	0.3588	0.6669

The data from the sensor was converted to g level based on the range of the sensor and the conversion factor from the SparkFun web site, which is $0.0078 \times$ value of the reading from the sensor. This data is displayed on a graph in Figure 6-30.

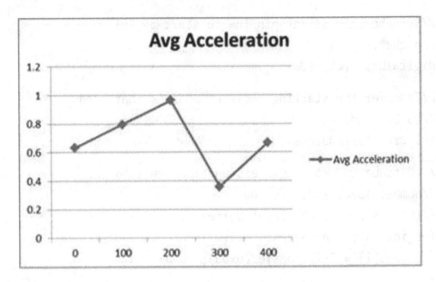

Figure 6-30. *Graph of Car Acceleration and Deceleration*

Acceleration Without Computer Recap

Figure 6-30 shows how acceleration ramps up quickly and then drops off even faster as the car starts slowing down. Why do you think this is? This is because the driver had to apply the brakes, and this along with road friction slows the car down faster than it accelerates.

Summary

This chapter provides a wide variety of projects that demonstrate various science and engineering aspects. The first set of projects show how heat is transferred inside an object or when air moves over an object. There is a project that shows how to simulate zero gravity along with a system to compare changes in frictional force of different materials. Finally, the last two projects allow the reader to measure the acceleration of a baseball bat or a car. All of these projects demonstrate aspects where one measurement is dependent on another variable. The Arduino, the Raspberry Pi, and these amazing sensors are excellent devices to capture this information just like the *Star Trek* tricorder.

CHAPTER 7

Light and Imaging Projects

The objective of this chapter is to gain insight into how light provides us with heat and when reflected off the moon or other celestial objects provides beautiful images. With regard to the latter, this chapter teaches novice astronomers how to develop a modern, automated imaging system for a telescope through two projects.

The first project demonstrates how to use an Arduino with a unique light sensor to gain an understanding of radiation heat transfer. The second project uses a Raspberry Pi and its camera to capture unique images to study the moon and several planets.

These concepts associated with light and imaging will provide inspiration and guidance for novice astronomers and heat transfer engineers, who would like to improve their ability to measure energy in light or capture images of the moon, planets, and other celestial points of interest.

Radiation Heat Transfer

Most of the heat comes to our planet from the sun via light and the radiation method of heat transfer. On a cold morning, it feels very nice to stand in the sunlight. There is a lot of heat energy in sunlight, and it is

© Paul Bradt and David Bradt 2020
P. Bradt and D. Bradt, *Science and Engineering Projects Using the Arduino and Raspberry Pi*,
https://doi.org/10.1007/978-1-4842-5811-8_7

mostly transmitted via the visible and infrared wavelengths of light. This project uses a very unique sensor along with the Arduino to measure both infrared and visible light.

Science   Develop an understanding of light and radiation heat transfer.

Technology/Engineering   Using the Arduino and a unique light sensor to capture light intensity.

Mathematics   Conversion of radiation data to Lux in the code and estimation of radiation heat transfer directly from the sun or through a window with a reflective coating.

This project utilizes a very unique new sensor from Adafruit, the TSL 2591. It uses two photodiodes to measure various wavelengths of light. One photodiode is sensitive to infrared only, and the other is sensitive to visible light, infrared, and the full spectrum of light. This incredibly low-cost device then compares and integrates those measurements to calculate Lux (which is defined as lumens/square meter) and outputs values for visible and infrared light.

The purpose of this experiment is to estimate how much heat via radiation from the sun is transferred into a house through a window.

The parts needed are

- Arduino Uno

- Adafruit light sensor, TSL 2591 luminosity sensor

- Window

- Optional: Reflective window covering material

- Miscellaneous wires and proto-board

Figures 7-1 and 7-2 show the system set up in front of a window for the purpose of measuring the radiation heat transfer with and without the window closed.

Figure 7-1. *Open Window*

Figure 7-2. *Closed Window*

Figure 7-3 shows the schematic and connections of the TSL 2591 light sensor to the Arduino.

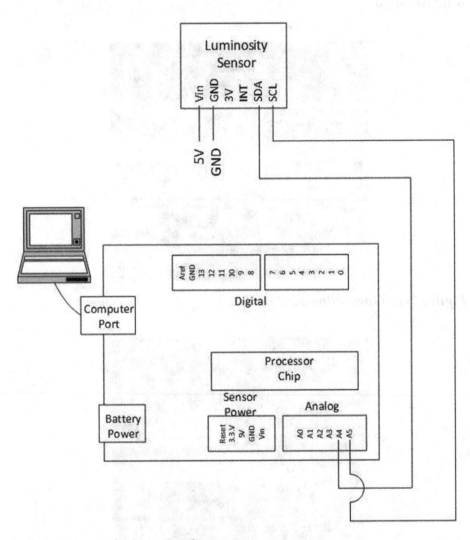

Figure 7-3. *Light Sensor Schematic*

Listing 7-1 has only very slight modifications to fit in this book. It is also configured to accept bright light. The new TSL 2591 sensor and this code work very well. It is a very amazing device to measure light in all kinds of conditions.

The Adafruit_Sensor.h and Adafruit_TSL2591.h libraries are needed for this code.

Note   The code that is bold below is on one line and should not overwrap when typed into the IDE.

Listing 7-1. Arduino SN108_TSL2591 Light Sensor Code

```
//SN108 minor modifications by Paul Bradt to
//Original code on Adafruit site
// TSL2591 Digital Light Sensor
// Dynamic Range: 600M:1
// Maximum Lux: 88K

#include <Wire.h>
#include <Adafruit_Sensor.h>
#include "Adafruit_TSL2591.h"

// Example for demonstrating the TSL2591 library -
// public domain!
// connect SCL to I2C Clock
// connect SDA to I2C Data
// connect Vin to 3.3-5V DC
// connect GROUND to common ground
Adafruit_TSL2591 tsl = Adafruit_TSL2591(2591);
// pass in a number for the sensor identifier (for
// your use later)
```

```
/*********************************************/

//Displays some basic information on this sensor
//from the unified sensor API sensor_t type (see
//Adafruit_Sensor for more information)

/*********************************************/
void displaySensorDetails(void)
  {
  sensor_t sensor;
  tsl.getSensor(&sensor);
  Serial.println(F("------------------------"));
  Serial.print  (F("Sensor:         "));
  Serial.println(sensor.name);
  Serial.print  (F("Driver Ver:   "));
  Serial.println(sensor.version);
  Serial.print  (F("Unique ID:    "));
  Serial.println(sensor.sensor_id);
  Serial.print  (F("Max Value:    "));
  Serial.print(sensor.max_value);
  Serial.println(F(" lux"));
  Serial.print  (F("Min Value:    "));
  Serial.print(sensor.min_value);
  Serial.println(F(" lux"));
  Serial.print  (F("Resolution:   "));
  Serial.print(sensor.resolution, 4);
  Serial.println(F(" lux"));
  Serial.println(F("------------------------"));
  Serial.println(F(""));
  delay(500);
}
```

```
/***********************************************/

//Configures the gain and integration time for the
//TSL2591

/***********************************************/
void configureSensor(void)
{
  // You can change the gain on the fly, to adapt to
  //brighter/dimmer light situations
  tsl.setGain(TSL2591_GAIN_LOW);//1x gain
  //(Use line above for bright light)
  //tsl.setGain(TSL2591_GAIN_MED);        // 25x gain
  //tsl.setGain(TSL2591_GAIN_HIGH);    // 428x gain

  // Changing the integration time gives you a longer
  //time over which to sense light
  // longer timelines are slower, but are good in
  // very low light situations!
  tsl.setTiming(TSL2591_INTEGRATIONTIME_100MS);
  // Use line above for bright light
  // shortest integration time (bright light)
  // tsl.setTiming(TSL2591_INTEGRATIONTIME_200MS);
  // tsl.setTiming(TSL2591_INTEGRATIONTIME_300MS);
  // tsl.setTiming(TSL2591_INTEGRATIONTIME_400MS);
  // tsl.setTiming(TSL2591_INTEGRATIONTIME_500MS);
  // tsl.setTiming(TSL2591_INTEGRATIONTIME_600MS);
  // longest integration time (dim light)

  //Display the gain and integration time for
  //reference sake
  Serial.println(F("---------------------------"));
  Serial.print  (F("Gain:         "));
  tsl2591Gain_t gain = tsl.getGain();
```

155

```
  switch(gain)
  {
    case TSL2591_GAIN_LOW:
      Serial.println(F("1x (Low)"));
      break;
    case TSL2591_GAIN_MED:
      Serial.println(F("25x (Medium)"));
      break;
    case TSL2591_GAIN_HIGH:
      Serial.println(F("428x (High)"));
      break;
    case TSL2591_GAIN_MAX:
      Serial.println(F("9876x (Max)"));
      break;
  }
  Serial.print  (F("Timing:       "));
  Serial.print((tsl.getTiming() + 1) * 100, DEC);
  Serial.println(F(" ms"));
  Serial.println(F("--------------------------------"));
  Serial.println(F(""));
}

/**********************************************/
/*

    Program entry point for the Arduino sketch
*/
/**********************************************/
void setup(void)
{
  Serial.begin(9600);

  Serial.println(F("Starting TSL2591 Test!"));
```

```
if (tsl.begin())
{
  Serial.println(F("Found a TSL2591 sensor"));
}
else
{
  Serial.println(F("No sensor found ?"));
  while (1);
}

/* Display some basic information on this sensor */
displaySensorDetails();

/* Configure the sensor */
configureSensor();

// Now we're ready to get readings ... move on to
//loop()!
}
/****************************************************/
//Shows how to perform a basic read on visible,
//full spectrum or infrared light (returns raw 16-
//bit ADC values)
/****************************************************/
void simpleRead(void)
{
  // Simple data read example. Just read the
  //infrared, fullspecrtrum diode
  // or 'visible' (difference between the two)
  //channels.
  // This can take 100-600 milliseconds! Uncomment
  //whichever of the following you want to read
  uint16_t x = tsl.getLuminosity(TSL2591_VISIBLE);
```

157

```
//uint16_t x =
//tsl.getLuminosity(TSL2591_FULLSPECTRUM);
//uint16_t x = tsl.getLuminosity(TSL2591_INFRARED);

  Serial.print(F("[ ")); Serial.print(millis());
  Serial.print(F(" ms ] "));
  Serial.print(F("Luminosity: "));
  Serial.println(x, DEC);
}

/**********************************************/
//Show how to read IR and Full Spectrum at once
//and convert to lux
/**********************************************/
void advancedRead(void)
{
  // More advanced data read example. Read 32 bits
  // with top 16 bits IR, bottom 16 bits full
  // spectrum.   That way you can do whatever math and
  //comparisons you want!
  uint32_t lum = tsl.getFullLuminosity();
  uint16_t ir, full;
  ir = lum >> 16;
  full = lum & 0xFFFF;
  Serial.print(F("[ ")); Serial.print(millis());
  Serial.print(F(" ms ] "));
  Serial.print(F("IR: ")); Serial.print(ir);
  Serial.print(F("  "));
  Serial.print(F("Full: ")); Serial.print(full);
  Serial.print(F("  "));
  Serial.print(F("Visible: "));
  Serial.print(full - ir);
```

```
  Serial.print(F("  "));
  Serial.print(F("Lux: "));
  Serial.println(tsl.calculateLux(full, ir), 6);
}

/**************************************************/
//Performs a read using the Adafruit Unified
//Sensor API.

/**************************************************/
void unifiedSensorAPIRead(void)
{
  /* Get a new sensor event */
  sensors_event_t event;
  tsl.getEvent(&event);

  //Display the results (light is measured in lux)
  Serial.print(F("[ "));
  Serial.print(event.timestamp);
  Serial.print(F(" ms ] "));
  if ((event.light == 0) |
      (event.light > 4294966000.0) |
      (event.light <-4294966000.0))
  {
    // If event.light = 0 lux the sensor is probably
    // saturated and no reliable data could be
    // generated!
    // if event.light is +/- 4294967040 there was a
    // float over/underflow
    Serial.println(F("Invalid adjust gain_timing"));
  }
  else
```

```
  {
    Serial.print(event.light);
    Serial.println(F(" lux"));
  }
}

/****************************************/
/****************************************/
void loop(void)
{
  //simpleRead();
  advancedRead();
  // unifiedSensorAPIRead();

  delay(500);
}
```

Table 7-1 shows the data captured on a sunny day. The raw visible and infrared light was captured with the window open, and then the data was observed when the window was closed. The window had a reflective film on it to reduce the light coming through it.

Table 7-1. *Example Radiation Heat Transfer Data*

Configuration	Avg IR	Avg Visible	Sum of IR + Visible	Improvement with Covering
Raw sunlight	1991	2772	4763	
Window w/ reflective covering	503	927	1430	70% reduction

Analysis of Heat Transfer

The authors then used the preceding data to develop an analysis of the heat transferred through a window. This can be used to do design trades of the number and size of windows. Another study could look at which direction a building or home faces and how many windows are located on the south-facing walls.

Start with the equation of the solar radiation hitting the Earth:

$$dq/dt = (1000 \text{ W/m}^2) \, \epsilon \, A \cos \Theta$$

For this experiment, the 1000 W/m² value will be adjusted based on the visible and infrared readings taken from the sensor:

$$dq/dt = (\text{Window Reduction Factor}) \, (1000 \text{ W/m}^2) \, \epsilon \, A \cos \Theta$$

where

> Window Reduction Factor = (1 -0.7) = 0.3 from observations
>
> ϵ = 0.96 for a white-painted surface
>
> A = 1 m² using a square meter which can easily be scaled up or down for larger or smaller areas

Assume a 30-degree incidence of light hitting the window.

Calculate the heat transfer for the window with reflective coating with reduction factor:

$$dq/dt = (0.30)\,(1000)\,(0.96)\,(1) \cos 30 = 249 \text{ watts for one m}^2$$

Calculate the heat transfer for the raw sunlight with no reduction factor:

$$dq/dt = (1000)\,(0.96)\,(1) \cos 30 = 831 \text{ watts for one m}^2$$

Taking this analysis one step further for a large house with six windows that are 2 m², the heat transfer rate would be, at this time of day with this angle of incidence, 6 × 2 × 831 watts, or approximately 10,000 watts. That is a lot of heat entering through those windows.

Adding the reflective coating reduces that to 3000 watts which is a lot less but still quite a bit of energy.

Engineers can use analysis like this to ensure the air-conditioning system is sized properly and provides adequate cooling on hot days.

Radiation Heat Transfer Recap

The preceding data shows how beneficial from a heat transfer perspective using windows with reflective coatings can be to reduce the amount of solar radiation (heat) that enters a window. It can also be utilized to estimate the amount of heat contribution and develop changes to the number and size of windows when designing a building or house.

Astrophotography with the Raspberry Pi Camera

This project shows another way to use sunlight as it is reflected off other planets which can be captured here on Earth using telescopes. This project also demonstrates an innovative concept and a great example of dedicating a low-cost Raspberry Pi to a permanent task by converting it into a modern astrophotographic machine. Figure 7-4 is one of the first images the authors captured with the Raspberry Pi 3 telescope system, and it just made them want to capture more examples.

Figure 7-4. *Image the Authors Captured of the Moon with Raspberry Pi and Telescope*

This final project shows how to attach the Raspberry Pi to some older telescopes to convert them to nice modern imaging machines. The first subsection shows how a Raspberry Pi camera system can be added to a Meade ETX-60AT telescope. This is a very nice little scope that has a controller and a drive system that will keep it tracking the object despite the Earth's rotation. The second subsection attaches the same Raspberry Pi camera system to a standard 4 ½-inch reflector telescope.

Science   Develop an understanding of astronomy, the moon, and planets.

Technology/Engineering   Using the Raspberry Pi and its camera along with telescopes to gather images of astronomical items. Planning and building a complex system. Learning how to use a 3D printer.

Mathematics   Develop an understanding of how mathematics is used to ensure multiple assemblies fit together.

STEM   This section is a great example of the difference between engineering and science. The majority of this section covers the engineering needed to develop this unique combination of modern

163

Raspberry Pi technology with two different older telescopes. These devices are then used by the scientist to explore astronomy, gather data, and capture beautiful images of the moon and the two largest planets.

The first subsections describe how to do the setup of the Meade ETX-60AT telescope and the 4 ½-inch reflector telescope. They also highlight the code that operates the cameras to take both still images and videos. The later subsections show how to build the components for these complex but very useful devices. In the "Appendix" section, there is information regarding the Meade ETX-60AT telescope. This telescope is no longer available from the manufacturer, but the reader may be able to obtain one on eBay or some other similar telescope.

Note   The section "Astrophotography with the Raspberry Pi Camera" is presented in reverse order; it may be confusing at first, but the reason for this is to help the reader understand the final goal first and then explain how the authors reached that goal. The objective of this project is to set up an astrophotography telescope system that is adaptable to different telescopes and easy to use.

The following is a list of the subsections, and the reader may want to jump around them based on their interest:

7.2.1: Assembling the Meade ETX-60AT and Raspberry Pi

7.2.2: Assembling the 4 ½-Inch Reflector Telescope and the Raspberry Pi

7.2.3: Basic Raspistill Previewing an Image with the Terminal Command Line

7.2.4: Astrophotography Raspberry Pi Python GUI

7.2.5: Assembling the Raspberry Pi and Touchscreen in the Case

7.2.6: Camera Modifications, Camera Case, and Power Cables

7.2.7: Building the Shelf for the Meade ETX-60AT

7.2.8: Helpful Hints Using the Telescope and Raspberry Pi

7.2.9: Example Images and Enhancing Them Using a Video Capture GUI

Assembling the Meade ETX-60AT and Raspberry Pi

The individual pieces (telescope, Raspberry Pi/touchscreen/case, and the shelf) have their own sections later that describe them. The following diagrams in this section show how the major pieces are assembled.

The authors tried to modularize the system so that it can quickly be assembled or disassembled. One unique feature of this design is the Raspberry Pi 3 system can be removed with one screw and set up as its own work station to review and select the pictures remotely from the telescope. Note that in the top view in Figure 7-5, the telescope and support yokes are not shown.

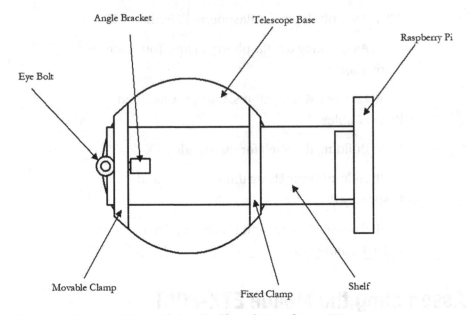

Figure 7-5. *Top View of the Shelf and Raspberry Pi*

Figure 7-6 shows the assembled system with identification labels for the components.

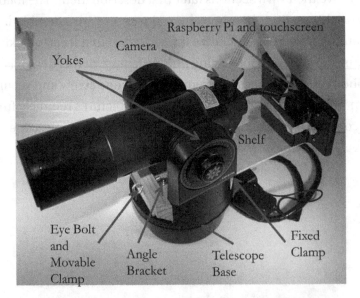

Figure 7-6. *Assembled Raspberry Pi, Shelf, and Telescope*

166

After all key components are built, the astronomer should follow these seven steps to assemble the system:

1. Insert AA batteries into the telescope (Figure 7-7) in accordance with the telescope instructions. Because of their location, under the shelf, the batteries need to be inserted first.

Figure 7-7. *Battery Installation in Meade Telescope*

2. Attach the Raspberry Pi 3 and case to the shelf (Figure 7-8).

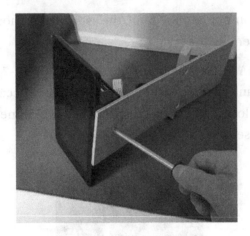

Figure 7-8. *Attaching Raspberry Pi to Shelf*

3. Slide the shelf through the telescope yoke (Figure 7-9).

4. Place the movable clamp against the front of the
    yoke and screw in the eye bolt through the movable
    clamp into the RIVNUT angle bracket (Figure 7-9).

5. Tighten the eye bolt until the clamp secures the
    shelf in place.

Figure 7-9. *Tightening the Clamp with the Eye Bolt*

6. Insert the Raspberry Pi 3 camera case into the
    telescope eyepiece (Figure 7-10).

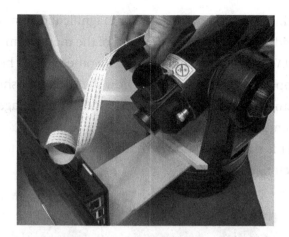

Figure 7-10. *Insert Pi Camera Case into Eyepiece*

7. Follow the Meade telescope setup instructions
    to enable star tracking. Now it is ready to start
    capturing beautiful images!

Astrophotography Meade ETX-60AT Setup Recap

The small size of the Meade ETX-60AT with the Raspberry Pi attached to it
is perfect for an amateur astronomer as it can be left set up. It has a small
footprint, takes a small space, and is ready to go at a moment's notice!

Assembling the 4 1/2-Inch Reflector Telescope and the Raspberry Pi

This section shows the same Raspberry Pi system mounted to a different
telescope using a body mount method. It uses a system that mounts the
Raspberry Pi 3 using a 5-inch hose clamp and a few pieces of ½ × 3/16-
inch wood to the body of the telescope tube. The Raspberry Pi 3 and
touchscreen were too heavy to body mount to the Meade ETX-60AT as the
motors were not strong enough to move it. However, it works very well on
this non-powered old reflector telescope.

The following images show the greater magnification a more powerful telescope provides compared to the images of the moon from the smaller Meade ETX-60AT. The authors included some other images here too from this old telescope and an explanation of how they accomplished them. Then enhancement is provided in the section "Example Images and Enhancing Them Using a Video Capture GUI."

Figure 7-11 is a beautiful image of the Sea of Serenity taken with the 4 ½-inch reflector.

Figure 7-11. *Moon: Sea of Serenity Image from 4 ½-Inch Reflector, April 8, 2018*

The next image, Figure 7-12, is of Saturn taken using this system.

Figure 7-12. *Saturn from 4 ½-Inch Reflector, April 11, 2018*

Figure 7-13 shows an image of Saturn that was taken from a video and processed per the steps listed in the section "Example Images and Enhancing Them Using a Video Capture GUI".

Figure 7-13. *Enhanced Saturn Image from 4 1/2-Inch Reflector, April 25, 2018*

Figure 7-14 is an image of Jupiter from a video that was taken with the 4 ½-inch reflector and enhanced using the techniques outlined in Section 7.2.9. It was the first time from this 40-year-old telescope the authors had been able to discern the great red spot!

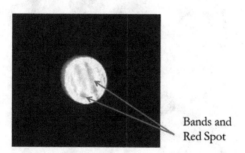

Bands and
Red Spot

Figure 7-14. *Enhanced Jupiter Image from 4 1/2-Inch Reflector, May 4, 2018*

Components Needed to Assemble the Raspberry Pi 3 Mounting System to the 4 1/2-Inch Telescope

This system is relatively simple and does not require as complex a system to mount the Raspberry Pi 3 as the Meade ETX-60AT telescope; see Figures 7-15 through 7-19 for details on the mounting system and that will allow attaching a Raspberry Pi to this older telescope.

Sighting this telescope on a distant planet like Saturn is a little difficult. The authors found it best to find it first with the eyepiece, then remove it, and insert the Raspberry Pi camera to get the image. Due to the Earth's rotation, the image moves rather quickly across the telescope's view, so the astronomer will need to install the Pi camera and take the image quickly.

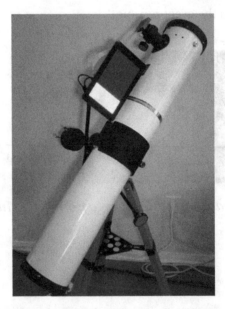

Figure 7-15. *4 1/2-Inch Reflector with Raspberry Pi*

Figure 7-16. *Hose Clamp for Body-Mounted Raspberry Pi 3*

Figure 7-17. *Close-Up of Body-Mounted Version*

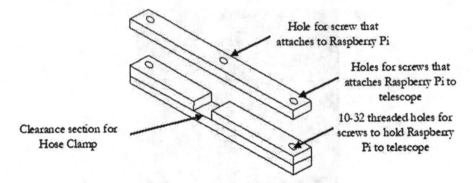

Hole for screw that
attaches to Raspberry Pi

Holes for screws that
attaches Raspberry Pi to
telescope

10-32 threaded holes for
screws to hold Raspberry
Pi to telescope

Clearance section for
Hose Clamp

Figure 7-18. *Body-Mounted Raspberry Pi System*

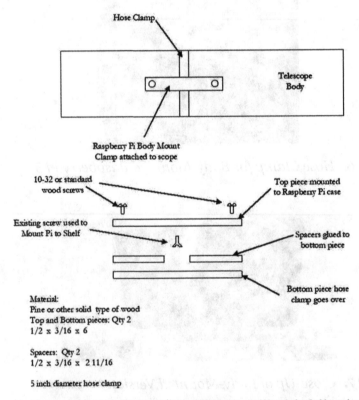

Hose Clamp

Telescope
Body

Raspberry Pi Body Mount
Clamp attached to scope

10-32 or standard
wood screws

Top piece mounted
to Raspberry Pi case

Existing screw used to
Mount Pi to Shelf

Spacers glued to
bottom piece

Bottom piece hose
clamp goes over

Material:
Pine or other solid type of wood
Top and Bottom pieces: Qty 2
1/2 x 3/16 x 6

Spacers: Qty 2
1/2 x 3/16 x 2 11/16

5 inch diameter hose clamp

Two screws: The authors used 10-32 x 1/2 screws, however they could be substitued with wood screws
just make sure they are not too long and extend through the top, spacers, and bottom pieces.

Figure 7-19. *Parts for the Body Mount System*

After adding the Raspberry Pi and camera, the 4 1/2-inch reflector telescope is now set up and ready to take some pictures of the larger planets.

Reflector Telescope Setup Recap

Turning these two older telescopes into modern astrophotography machines was a real joy. The next sections detail first a simple method without programing to start taking images. Later sections detail how to program two GUIs for easy picture and video captures. The final sections provide details on building the complex shelf set up to attach the Raspberry Pi to the Meade ETX-60AT.

Basic Raspistill Previewing an Image with the Terminal Command Line

If the reader is not interested in programming the Raspberry Pi, these first methods using built-in tools and simple commands in the terminal are perfect for using the system right away. Later sections provide code that creates a nice GUI. One other use for Raspistill is to test the Raspberry Pi camera and the telescope system to make sure it is functioning before starting to work on the GUI described in later sections.

The first method that the authors used to capture images is the onboard program named Raspistill. Todd Franke provided the info on how to use this very useful tool.

Using Raspistill requires a keyboard to type in commands in the terminal program command line. This is very similar to using the old DOS program line. Using a keyboard is a little awkward when the scope is outside and it's dark. Functionally however, the program works very well. See Figure 7-20 for the terminal input.

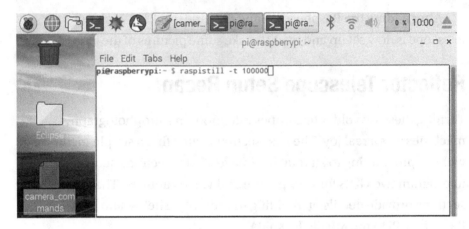

Figure 7-20. *Raspistill Typed into Terminal Command Line*

Figure 7-20 previews an image for an extended period of time. In this example, the program previews images for 100,000 milliseconds (i.e., 100 seconds) or a little more than 1 1/2 minutes. If you just want to show the image to others, this might be a nice long view.

The preview length shown at the top of the screen to the right uses the following command:

Raspistill -t 100000.

If the astronomer is planning to take a number of photos, this might be too long, and the time can be shortened. If no time is specified, it previews for 5 seconds.

Note   Having the preview for an extended period is a great way to focus the telescope. In the case of the Meade telescope, the focus knob is at the end of the body tube and moves the front lens forward and backward.

Using Raspistill to Capture an Image

Another way to use Raspistill is to capture an image. The following needs to be typed into the terminal command line:

```
raspistill -o cam.jpg
```

Raspberry Pi 3 saves an image with the name cam.jpg. The following site provides additional information regarding using Raspistill including how to add a time stamp to the image captured:

www.raspberrypi.org/documentation/usage/camera/raspicam/
raspistill.md

More Advanced Raspistill Input Without a Keyboard

The authors also came up with a way to input the commands using only a mouse. This is a lot less awkward outside at night during an observation session. It requires some setup time prior to the observation session. The astronomer uses either the simple text editor or a program on the Pi called Libre Word Processor. Use these programs to set up the Raspistill commands in a file. Using only a mouse, the astronomer can open the document file and then highlight, copy, and paste the text command into the command line. This capability simplifies and reduces commanding time. The no-keyboard configuration may also make it easier to operate outside during an observation session.

One important trick to make this work is inserting a return or a line break at the end of the line of code. The astronomer is able to shorten the time it takes to use the Raspistill commands by typing them in by performing the following steps:

1. Save the document on the Raspberry Pi desktop.

2. Open the document.

3. Open the terminal command line.

4. Copy and paste the line and the line break into the command line in the terminal program.

The results of these steps can be seen in Figure 7-21.

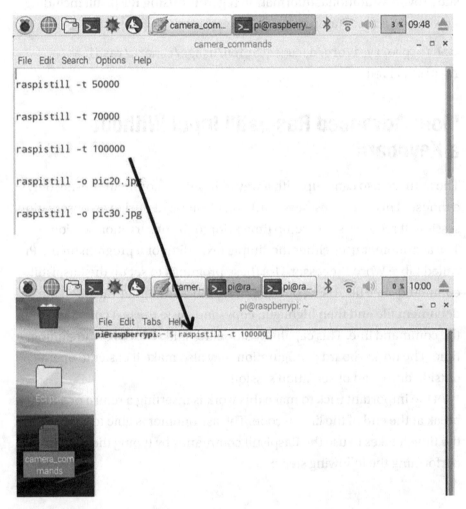

Figure 7-21. *Copy and Paste Commands into Script Line*

The authors used these stored commands:

```
raspistill - t 70000

raspistill -t 10000

raspistill -o pic20.jpg

raspistill -o pic30.jpg
```

The first two of these commands turn the preview on for 10,000 or 70,000 milliseconds, which is equivalent to 10 or 70 seconds. The 70 seconds is probably needed to focus the object. The 10 seconds is enough to look quickly before taking a picture and to ensure the object is still in view or in focus. The next two commands take a picture. It names the file image pic20.jpg or pic30.jpg.

The astronomer will need to change the file name or move these files from the Raspberry Pi, or the Raspistill will overwrite them the next time you run these lines of code.

The astronomer can insert his/her own code into the command file if some other name is desired.

Raspistill Image Capture Recap

Since the Raspberry Pi is a full-blown computer, there are already built-in tools that the reader can access and use. If the reader would like to automate taking images, the next section provides code to develop a GUI using the built-in Tkinter module.

Astrophotography Raspberry Pi Python GUI

The authors wanted to minimize working on coding, yet provide an easy way to operate the Raspberry Pi 3 camera and functionally provide great images, such as that shown in Figure 7-4. There are sites that provide excellent information regarding GUIs and the Raspberry Pi 3 camera, and they can aid in minimizing programming and provide useful and easy methods to operate the telescope with a Raspberry Pi 3. For other astronomers who are interested in more intricate or elaborate coding, there are sites that may provide starting points to develop their own version.

The following site provides the astronomer with a good basic understanding of how to set up a GUI to command the Raspberry Pi 3 to perform a desired function and was the starting point for the authors' code in Listing 7-2:

`http://robotic-controls.com/learn/python-guis/basics-tkinter-gui`

This site contains a very impressive GUI design for operating the Raspberry Pi camera, for those who want to adjust and manipulate the image:

`www.raspberrypi.org/forums/viewtopic.php?t=47857`

The authors chose a more modest path and created the following code that runs in Tkinter and uses the Pi camera program to capture and display the images shown in this book. Figure 7-22 shows this very straightforward GUI. It reminds the authors of the view screen on the bridge of the Enterprise in the *Star Trek in the original series TV shows*!

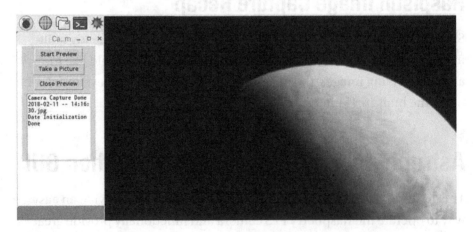

Figure 7-22. *GUI for Raspberry Pi Camera*

The code shown in Listing 7-2 has three main parts:

1. The first part is setting up the Tkinter main window and camera basic functions.

2. The second part of the program initializes the widgets that run the commands when you click the buttons.

3. The third part configures how the window should look. Once that is complete, root.main loop () starts up the program and will not run or load anything after that point.

The faint numbers are line numbers for the code; they need to be deleted if the reader copies this code. Be sure that the indention for the program is identical to what is shown in the following. The indention is how the Python compiler knows what is in scope or not.

Listing 7-2. Raspberry Pi Code PI_SN003_Astrophotograhy_Image Capture

```
0 #Code Developed by Paul Bradt
1 import tkinter as tk
2 import picamera
3 import os
4 import traceback
5 import datetime
6 import time
7 import sys
8 pwd = os.getcwd()
9 root = tk.Tk() #makes the window
10 root.geometry('200x1100+0+0')# Z x Y is how big window is
   and +0+0 is where window starts
11 camera = picamera.PiCamera()
```

```
12 root.wm_title("Camera GUI Program") #Makes the title that
   will appear      in the top left
13 root.config(background = "#FFFFFF") #Sets background color
   to white
14 #put widgets here
15 def previewcapture():
16                camera.start_preview (fullscreen=False,window
                  = (200,0,1100,640))
17 def picapture():
18      try:
19              now = datetime.datetime.now().strftime
                ("%F -- %X") + '.jpg'
20            debugLog.insert(0.0, "Date Initialization Done\n")
21            debugLog.insert(0.0, now + "\n")
22            time.sleep(5)
23            camera.capture(now, format = 'jpeg')
24            debugLog.insert(0.0, "Camera Capture Done\n")
25      except:
26              print(traceback.format_exc( limit=10))
27 def stopcapture():
28      camera.stop_preview()
29 #Main Frame and its contents
30 mainFrame = tk.Frame(root, width=200, height = 900)
31 mainFrame.grid(row=0, column=1, padx=10, pady=2)
32 btnFrame = tk.Frame(mainFrame, width=200, height = 200)
33 btnFrame.grid(row=1, column=0, padx=10, pady=2)
34 debugLog = tk.Text(mainFrame, width = 20, height = 10, takefocus=0)
35 debugLog.grid(row=3, column=0, padx=10, pady=2)
36 previewBtn = tk.Button(btnFrame, text="Start Preview",
   command=previewcapture)
37 previewBtn.grid(row=0, column=0, padx=10, pady=2)
```

```
38 cameraBtn = tk.Button(btnFrame, text="Take a Picture",
   command=picapture)
39 cameraBtn.grid(row=1, column=0, padx=10, pady=2)
40 stopBtn = tk.Button(btnFrame, text="Close Preview",
   command=stopcapture)
41 stopBtn.grid(row=2, column=0, padx=10, pady=2)
42 root.mainloop() #start monitoring and updating the
   GUI. Nothing  below here runs.
```

The light-gray numbers at the start of the line represent the line of code and are not in the program.

Make sure this code is saved in a file as "your file name here.py" for Python and saved in the main folder.

Initiating the GUI

1. Open Programming and then open Python.

2. Open the file that contains the preceding program.

3. Open Run and then Run module.

The authors learned these tips and tricks while developing this code.

If for some reason the window does not show up, it may be outside the view of the monitor. The following part of the code

```
root.geometry('200x1100+0+0')
```

sets the location of the GUI at 200 × 1100 pixel sizes. It is the window size, and +0+0 is the x–y position using pixels again. The code may need to be adjusted to move the location to a different one. The authors wrote this code to match the 7-inch touchscreen. For other monitor sizes, the programmer may need to change the position and size to fit.

The authors found that the touchscreen can be used to take a picture, but it might set up a vibration and potentially blur the image. Using a wireless mouse prevented that from happening.

PI_SN003 Raspberry PI GUI Recap

This program PI_SN003 is very easy to use during an observation session. It lets you observe the object constantly, and then when the perfect image appears, with a simple click of the mouse you capture a fantastic image!

Assembling the Raspberry Pi and Touchscreen in the Case

There is a bit of engineering required to develop the system that connects the Raspberry Pi to the Meade ETX-60AT. The first part is the housing and touchscreen which is a nice package for the system. The second part shows how to 3D print the Pi camera case. The final part is the shelf bracket that grips the telescope and holds the Raspberry Pi/touchscreen assembly.

Raspberry Pi, Touchscreen, and Case

This section describes the assembly of the Raspberry Pi, touchscreen, and housing for them. One of the key features for this project is the touchscreen to show the image to ensure it is in focus. The 7-inch screen is an excellent choice for this application, as it is large with good contrast and definition. The authors found a case they liked that nicely integrated the touchscreen and the Raspberry Pi 3. It was also easy to modify the case with a single hole and add a RIVNUT to attach it to the shelf.

The parts needed are

- Raspberry Pi 3 Model B (≈$25)

- Raspberry Pi 7-inch touchscreen (≈$80)

- Raspberry Pi camera V2 (≈$30)

- Premium case for Raspberry Pi 7-inch touchscreen (≈$17); Digi-key part#: ASM-1900035-21

- Camera cable, 12 inches long (≈$2)

- Two 5-volt Raspberry Pi power supplies with a micro-USB connector (≈2 × $7.50)

- Cable wrap to combine power supply cords ($3)

- 8-32 RIVNUT

- 8-32 × ¾ flat head screw

Total cost ≈ $185

For remote operations where there is no power, the reader may want to use a power inverter. It is a device that plugs into a lighter connection in a car and changes the DC to AC and can power the Raspberry Pi and touchscreen. The authors needed this device to capture the eclipse images. The model used was the remote operations power inverter ($35), Wagan Tech part number: SmartAC 200 USB+.

Modification of the Case and Assembly

The authors made two modifications to the Raspberry Pi 3 case. The first is drilling a hole so that the RIVNUT could be attached. A RIVNUT, as seen in Figure 7-23, is a unique device which is installed like a rivet and therefore is locked to the housing. Internally, it has female threads so that a screw can be threaded into it. The installation procedure is shown in Figure 7-24.

Figure 7-23. *RIVNUT*

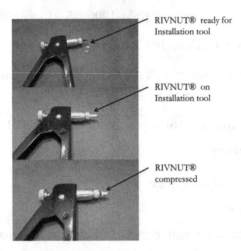

Figure 7-24. *RIVNUT Installation Procedure*

Figure 7-25 shows it installed in the Raspberry Pi touchscreen case.

Figure 7-25. *RIVNUT Installed in the Case*

An alternative to the RIVNUT approach is to simply glue a small nut inside the case using epoxy. This should be adequate to apply enough torque to secure the Raspberry Pi to the shelf.

One other important aspect is to apply tape over the end of the RIVNUT. This will catch any potential metal shavings when the screw is threaded into the case, clamping it down. Metal shavings could potentially short out circuit paths or connections which could damage the Raspberry Pi.

The second modification was gluing a small piece of plastic to the inside of the case to aid in restraining the ribbon cable as it twists to exit the case; this can be seen in Figure 7-26.

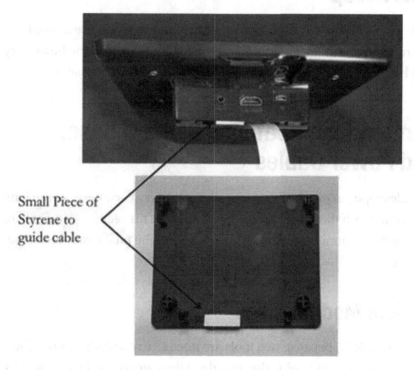

Small Piece of Styrene to guide cable

Figure 7-26. *Modification to the Case Backplate*

As a reminder, the touchscreen and case the authors selected result in the image being upside down initially. The following command must be added to the CONFIG.TXT file:

```
lcd_rotate=2
```

The case comes with instructions regarding this modification to the Raspberry Pi 3 setup.

Components and Assembly of the Raspberry Pi Case Recap

This case was perfect for this application; it had a great place to use for mounting to the shelf and contained the touchscreen and the Raspberry Pi. It has been used on many observation outings with no issues.

Camera Modifications, Camera Case, and Power Cables

The telescope becomes the lens for the Raspberry Pi camera, so the lens that comes with the camera must be removed. This section also describes making the camera case using 3D printing and the final assembly of the camera/case.

Camera Modifications

It is a little tricky, because two tools are needed to carefully remove the lens. One set of pliers holds the outside of the camera, and then the lens must be rotated out with forceps or another small tool (Figure 7-27).

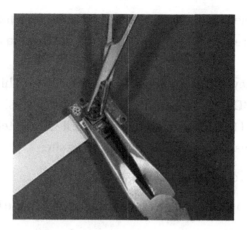

Figure 7-27. *Removing the Lens from Pi Camera*

Building the Camera Case

3D printing is an awesome technique that provides a unique way to create many different shaped parts. This is similar to the replicators in the original *Star Trek* series. Many creator spaces online can help a person develop parts using the 3D printing process. Mitch Long was very helpful in showing the authors how to create these camera cases.

The first step is to use computer-aided design (CAD) software to create a virtual model. The next step is to load that model in the correct format into the 3D printer, which uses a device that heats a material so that it flows easily. It precisely controls laying the melted material, layer upon layer, leaving voids in accordance with the input model, and gradually shaping the object until completion in each dimension. Hence, the process actually creates a 3D hardware object using a procedure that is partially analogous to ordinary paper printing.

The authors used a CAD program (see Appendix) to design and build the Raspberry Pi camera case. They output it in an STL format and took that (Figures 7-28 to 7-31) to a local library that had a 3D printer (MakerBot Replicator2). In about an hour, the basic part was completed.

The authors then drilled and tapped four holes for a flat cover plate as illustrated in Figures 7-32, 7-33, and 7-34, and the camera case was nearly ready to be used.

The authors have uploaded their Pi camera case to Thingiverse, which is a repository of 3D files. The authors created both a version for the Meade ETX-60AT (1 ¼-inch diameter) and the 4 ½-inch telescope (1-inch diameter). The files are located at the following site:

www.thingiverse.com/thing:2885450

Figure 7-28 shows the image of the camera case in the CAD program.

Figure 7-28. *Camera Case for Raspberry Pi, Ready for 3D Printing*

The dimensions for the camera case are shown in Figure 7-29.

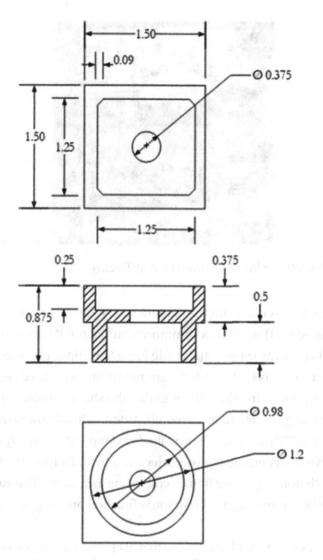

Figure 7-29. *3D Printed Camera Case (Dimensions in Inches)*

Note   Drawings in this book may not be to scale.

The camera case is starting to take shape in Figure 7-30.

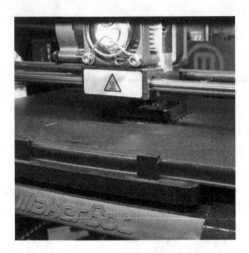

Figure 7-30. *3D Printer: Camera Case Taking Shape*

The material used to print the camera case was standard black PLA (polylactic acid) which is a common material for 3D printers. The MakerBot slicer software sets up the file for 3D printing. The slicer software used by the authors is CURA. A few parameters are set that relate to the fill and the supports. To minimize material, the shape is mostly hollow. The fill percentage creates a honeycomb structure inside the shape. The authors set it at 20% since it will be drilled and tapped. Typically the fill is set at 10%. Another setting that was selected is to add supports; these keep a section with nothing under it from collapsing as it cools. The supports will need to be removed after the shape is finished printing as seen in Figure 7-31.

If the reader does not have access to a 3D printer, there are several companies that will (for a fee) print out an object. Shapeways is one: www.shapeways.com.

Figure 7-31. *Cleaning Up the 3D Printed Camera Case*

Figure 7-31 shows how the case comes from the printer and the items that need to removed. The first step is to remove what is called the raft. It is the plate that the 3D printer puts down first and ensures the print has a solid base to prevent warping. The next step is to remove the supports which were located in the square box of the camera case.

To finish the camera case, cut a small styrene sheet (0.030 inches thick) of plastic 1 ½ × 1 ½ inches square (Figure 7-32). Draw lines that guide where the holes will be drilled. If you use the authors' 3D case on Thingiverse, the holes should be approximately 0.095 inches in from the edge.

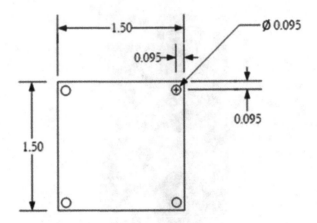

Figure 7-32. *Camera Case Cover (Dimensions in Inches)*

Tape the cover in place on the camera case (Figure 7-33) and drill through the cover plate, keeping the drill bit perpendicular to the plate. When the drill penetrates the cover plate, it leaves a mark where the hole will be drilled in the case. The reader can use extra 2-56 tap drill bits to help with alignment by placing them in each hole as it is drilled to keep the parts lined up. Otherwise, make sure the tape keeps the plate from shifting when drilling the next hole.

The authors cut a small notch in the cover and the case to guide the assembly. This is done while the tape is still in place and helps to ensure the cover can be placed in the correct orientation later, so that the holes line up properly after the tape is removed. Tap the holes using a 2-56 tap. Then the last modification is to file a slight gap for the camera cable to pass through. See Figures 7-33 and 7-34.

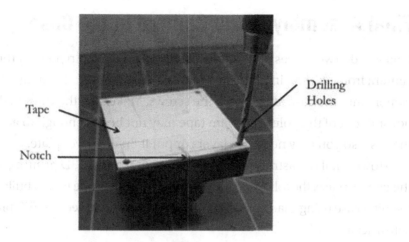

Figure 7-33. *Drilling Screw Holes in the Camera Case*

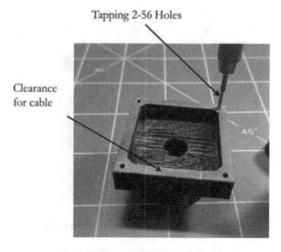

Figure 7-34. *Tapping the Screw Holes in the Camera Case*

Final Assembly of the Camera in the Case

Finally, add two pieces of double-sided foam tape to help prevent the camera from shifting in the case (Figures 7-35 and 7-36). Then insert the camera into the case and tighten the screws. Make sure the camera does not shift out of the hole. The foam tape may not be tall enough to adhere to the case, so you may need two layers or put it on the cover plate.

However, if the astronomer does not want to utilize 3D printing for the camera case, the following web site describes a unique way to build up a similar case using a large modified SD card case and a piece of PVC pipe to construct it:

www.instructables.com/id/Raspberry-Pi-Astro-Cam/

Foam Tape

Figure 7-35. *Foam Tape on Raspberry Pi Camera*

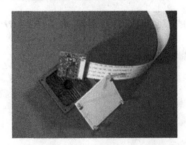

Figure 7-36. *Final Assembly of Camera into Case*

Power Cord Combination

The final aspect is a modification the authors made to the Raspberry Pi astrophotography system after using it for a short time. There are two power cables: one for the Raspberry Pi and the other for the touchscreen. They were constantly getting tangled up. The authors decided to wrap the two power cables with the slit cable wrap. This effectively created one power cable. See Figure 7-37. It significantly improved setup and cord entanglement issues.

Figure 7-37. *Power Cable Wrap*

Camera, Camera Case, and Power Cord Assembly Recap

This section outlines all of the changes needed to set up and assemble these key components for the Raspberry Pi astrophotography system.

Building the Shelf for the Meade ETX-60AT

This section describes the steps needed to construct the shelf assembly which contains the clamping device that provides a secure mounting place for the Raspberry Pi to the Meade ETX-60AT telescope. The shelf assembly makes a self-contained, easily transported setup for the telescope and

Raspberry Pi combination. This shelf requires a bit of woodworking skills, but each step is described. It provides the base for mounting the Raspberry Pi on and then using a clamp system that attaches it to Meade ETX-60AT. Building this requires a bit of engineering skills, using mathematics to lay out the hole patterns, and some manufacturing skills to fabricate the parts. Each section shows the steps required to build each part. There are four main parts: the shelf, fixed clamp, movable clamp, and eye screw/bracket (see Figures 7-38 and 7-39).

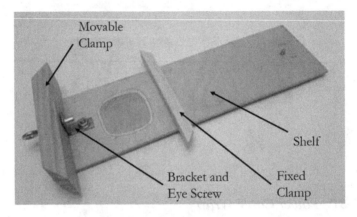

Figure 7-38. *Assembled Shelf*

The shelf assembly is made up of the subassemblies shown in Figure 7-39. Each component will be described in detail in the next few sections. It may look somewhat complex, but it is really straightforward.

As always, **safety first** when using saws and tools, especially if the reader is not familiar with their operation. Remember to use hearing protection and safety glasses when using power tools such as saws and drills. Inexperienced young astronomers should get assistance from an adult or visit a maker group. These are groups around the country and are set up to aid people who want to learn how to make things.

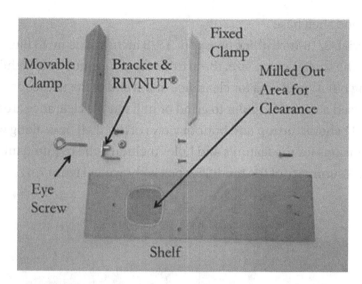

Figure 7-39. *Shelf Pieces*

Figure 7-40 shows the two areas that due to rotation of the scope to the vertical (overhead viewing) position may need some clearance added to the shelf and the fixed clamp. The authors did this, but the reader may find it unnecessary.

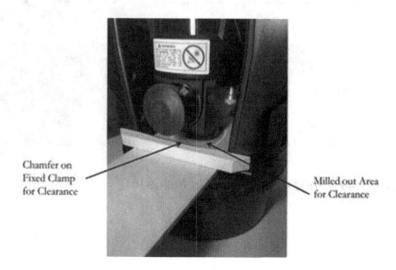

Figure 7-40. *Areas Modified to Ensure Clearance*

199

Plywood shelf base

Material: 3/16-inch-thick plywood, 3 5/8 inches wide by 13 inches long

After the shelf is cut to size, the astronomer must modify it slightly by milling out a small area for clearance of the end of the telescope. The authors used a Dremel grinder to grind or mill out the clearance area. Figure 7-41 shows the top and bottom views of the shelf base along with the dimensions for the features and holes including the required milled-out area. A summary of the modifications is shown in Figure 7-41.

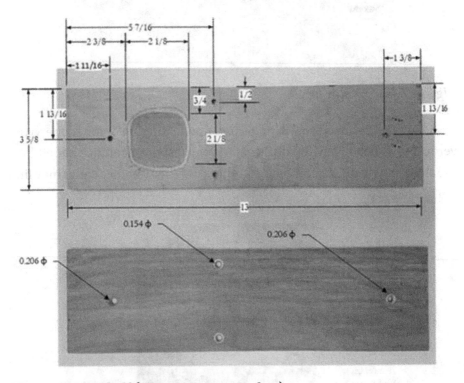

Figure 7-41. *Shelf (Dimensions in Inches)*

1. Mill out area for clearance.

2. One Raspberry Pi mounting hole.

3. Two holes for the fixed clamp.

4. One hole for the RIVNUT/bracket.

The authors used flat head screws so the holes must be countersunk on the shelf bottom.

Using the Dremel grinder tool, grind or mill out the clearance area, which is approximately 2 1/8 inches square and approximately 1/16–3/32 inches deep.

Fixed clamp (Figure 7-42)

Material: 1/2-inch square wood that is 5 1/2 inches long

Figure 7-42. *Fixed Clamp*

Summary of the modifications (See Figure 7-42):

1. Cut the ends at a 45-degree angle.

2. Chamfer one edge for clearance for telescope rotation.

3. Drill clearance holes for screws that are 2 1/8 inches apart and match the two holes in the shelf where the fixed clamp is attached.

Movable clamp (Figure 7-43)

Material: 1 ½ × 2 ½ × 5 ½-inch wood

Figure 7-43. Movable Clamp

Summary of the modifications (See Figure 7-43):

1. Cut the ends at a 45-degree angle.

2. One hole was drilled that matches the height of the RIVNUT/bracket.

The hole needs to be positioned so the movable clamp is slightly above and not resting on the shelf, so it does not drag when the eye bolt is tightened.

Bracket and RIVNUT (Figure 7-44)

Material: 1 inch × 1 inch angle bracket and RIVNUT

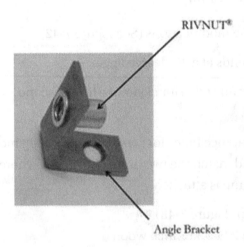

Figure 7-44. Angle Bracket with RIVNUT

Summary of the modifications (See Figure 7-44):

1. The hole in the bracket may need to be enlarged slightly for the RIVNUT to fit through prior to being expanded.

2. Install and expand RIVNUT in the same manner completed for the Raspberry Pi case.

Shelf Components and Assembly Recap

This section provides details on how to fabricate and assemble the shelf and the interfaces between the telescope and the Raspberry Pi. It makes a nice integrated package and is easy to assemble.

Helpful Hints Using the Telescope and Raspberry Pi

When the authors started using the astro-Pi telescope, they learned a few tricks and techniques that may be helpful to astronomers and science buffs:

1. Always make sure the telescope lens, camera, and the mirror are clean from debris, so that the astronomer captures a good clean image. The authors had several beautiful pictures ruined because of debris on the mirror that sends the image to the eyepiece.

2. If possible, plan ahead and position needed items for easy access. A table, power cords, and a flashlight are very helpful. Also, have the keyboard handy just in case you need to type in commands. The authors had to reboot the Raspberry Pi 3 during one observation session, because it locked up. They resorted to typing in the commands again.

3. If the astronomer copies and pastes commands into the script line, the authors recommend using the simple text editor rather than the word processor. The text editor seems more robust for setting this up, but you need to press "Enter" at the end of the line and make sure that you copy and paste this keystroke into the script.

4. Chairs for the astronomer and any other viewers make this an enjoyable experience.

5. To protect the touchscreen, the authors left the protective film on it. It did not seem to affect the functionality of the touchscreen and image quality, and it protected it from many bumps and potential scratches that occurred during assembly and use of the scope.

6. When doing the Autostar alignment of the Meade telescope, the authors found it helpful to cover the Raspberry Pi 3 screen with a cloth, because it is so bright that it makes it hard to see where the scope is pointing.

7. The authors sometimes accepted the Autostar alignment without verifying it through the eyepiece. If the telescope was in the general direction toward a bright star, then they accepted it. The fine alignment was done on the moon by loosening the yoke and adjusting it by hand.

8. The batteries for the Meade telescope tended to last no more than two or three observation sessions. It may appear as if it is working, but there may not be enough power to operate the motors in the

upright yokes. The scope will rotate horizontally, but not vertically. If the astronomer does a lot of observing, she/he may want to invest in two sets of rechargeable batteries, always prepared to swap out discharged with charged batteries.

9. The authors used a power inverter to power the Raspberry Pi for a remote location. Make sure the configuration is tested before going remote, as it may or may not be able to supply enough current to drive the Raspberry Pi 3 and touchscreen.

    The astronomer may want to try to power the Raspberry Pi 3 and touchscreen from a battery pack. The following web site explains how the astronomer may want to accomplish this goal. The site indicates the screen requires 500 mA and the Raspberry Pi draws 2.5 amps:

    `https://raspberrypi.stackexchange.com/questions/49533/powering-the-pi-3-model-b-with-a-battery-pack`

    On one remote observation session, the authors powered the Pi using an inverter plugged into the car. The inverter supplied a little over 2 amps, but had some surge capability. It worked fine and ran the system during one observation session for about an hour.

10. When focusing the Meade telescope, the primary lens moves up and down the barrel. As an aid, the authors put a piece of tape on the barrel and marked the location close to the normal focus for the moon. This helped to speed up focusing the scope during an observation session.

11. The astronomer may want to do a screen capture at some point. For the Raspberry Pi 3, the command typed into the terminal program is "scrot," and it will save the image in the main folder with date and time info in the file name.

12. An important lesson the authors learned is that the Raspberry Pi 3 power supply needs to deliver the amount of current required. The authors used one official Raspberry Pi 3 power supply and one random spare supply. It turned out that spare one would not deliver enough current to the Pi. It worked well for the touchscreen monitor. The system would crash often if the wrong power supply was used to power the Raspberry Pi 3. This caused a lot of challenges until the cause of the crashes was determined and corrected.

13. A wireless mouse eliminated one cable and made the system easier to use outside. The touchscreen can be used to activate the "take picture" button on the GUI, but the astronomer may cause a vibration or other movement when using it and potentially blur the image.

14. The authors had some challenges using a flash drive with the Raspberry Pi. It may be caused by the configuration. Normally the files are not too large, so it is easy to email the images. The authors used Gmail to do this on the Pi.

15. The authors found it very helpful to have a program on their personal computer that helps identify the location of the planets and stars. The program Stellarium, used by the authors, is an open source free code that does a great job: http://stellarium.org/.

16.   The authors found the following helpful site while
researching this project, which contains a lot of
great images and information about the moon:
www.alanchuhk.com/.

This book does not focus on how to take videos using this system, but
there are real benefits for image enhancement using a video. One way to
obtain a video is using the program Raspivid which works in a similar way
to Raspistill.

Lessons Learned Recap

After several observation sessions, the authors learned several lessons they
wanted to pass on to the reader. These items help to make a fun successful
observation session and can improve the experience for everyone involved.

Example Images and Enhancing Them Using a Video Capture GUI

The authors also developed a GUI that will take a video (the code is shown
later in this chapter). It is a modification to the authors' camera GUI. It will
create a video file with a unique file format that will need to be converted
to standard formats. This is described after the video GUI code.

If the astronomer becomes very interested in cleaning up the images,
there is a protocol called Planetary Image Pre-processing and image
stacking. It requires a video file and does an amazing job of overlapping
and correcting images. There is a short overview of these techniques later
in this chapter, but significant detail is beyond the scope of this book. The
authors thank Jeff Dunehew for providing the process to use videos to
create enhanced images. As the astronomer gains skills with their system,
this amazing technology can be explored.

Example Images Taken with the Upgraded Meade ETX-60AT Astrophotography System

The image in Figure 7-45 was taken when the temperature outside was 32 degrees Fahrenheit, and the Raspberry Pi 3 worked well. The crater details near the terminator are fascinating. With a little math, the astronomer might be able to determine a rough height for the crater wall given the known diameter of the moon.

Figure 7-45. *Moon on January 13, 2018*

Figure 7-46, taken early morning on January 29, 2018, clearly shows Jupiter and three of its moons. One unique historical fact regarding the Jovian moons is that Galileo used them to reason that the Earth orbited the sun. Over time he observed the paths of Jupiter's moons with respect to the planet. They were not stationary, and the only way he could explain those positional changes was orbital paths around Jupiter. Once he understood the orbital hierarchy of objects in the solar system, he reasoned that a similar orbital path existed in the Earth/sun relationship.

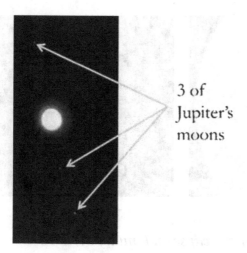

3 of
Jupiter's
moons

Figure 7-46. *Jupiter and Its Three Moons on January 29, 2018*

With the Raspberry Pi attached to the telescope, you too can capture sequential images over time and observe phenomena such as the motion of Jupiter's moons as they orbit the planet just like Galileo.

This set of images (Figure 7-47) of the lunar eclipse was taken on January 31, 2018, just as the moon was setting. It exemplifies time-lapse photography as it shows the progression of the eclipse in approximately 10-minute increments. One item of note that can be seen in the images is the terminator line is not very sharp. Compared to normal phased moon images, the terminator here appears "fuzzy." In a lunar eclipse, as the Earth passes between the sun and moon, particles in the Earth's atmosphere degrade the sun's light before it strikes the moon and produce the fuzzy nature of the terminator.

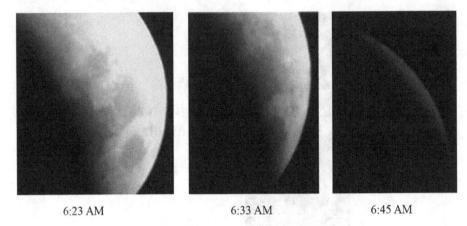

| 6:23 AM | 6:33 AM | 6:45 AM |

Figure 7-47. *Lunar Eclipse on January 31, 2018*

The next photo is of a full moon that occurred on March 1, 2018 (See Figure 7-48). It is pieced together from individual sections, as the whole moon does not fit in the screen.

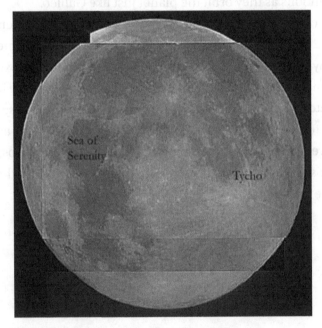

Figure 7-48. *Full Moon on March 1, 2018*

Using an image such as this, the astronomer can start finding and labeling craters and features on the moon they observe.

Finally, one more image, Figure 7-49, taken with the Meade ATX-60AT, was of a full moon on April 19, 2019. It shows the southern region very nicely and the crater Tycho.

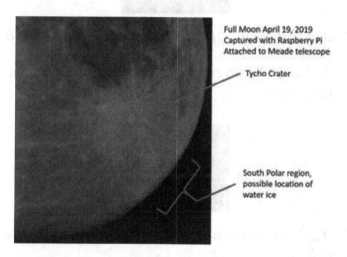

Full Moon April 19, 2019
Captured with Raspberry Pi
Attached to Meade telescope

Tycho Crater

South Polar region,
possible location of
water ice

Figure 7-49. *Full Moon on April 19, 2019, Southern Region*

Example Images Taken with the Upgraded 4 1/2-Inch Reflector Telescope Astrophotography System

The photos in this section were taken with the 4 ½-inch reflector using the body mount method previously described. It was a 40-year-old reflector telescope! There are some blemishes on the mirror, but they don't impact the image. The tripod and vernier controls still work well.

Making an Astronomical Video and Creating Enhanced Images

The following images (Figures 7-50 to 7-52) are repeated to demonstrate how an image can be enhanced using the video GUI Python program and the steps outlined later in this section.

Figure 7-50 is unenhanced image and 7-51 is after enhancement.

Figure 7-50. *Saturn from 4 1/2-Inch Reflector, April 11, 2018*

Figures 7-51 and 7-52 are enhanced images using the techniques outlined in this section.

Figure 7-51. *Enhanced Saturn Image from 4 1/2-Inch Reflector, April 25, 2018*

Figure 7-52 is the enhanced image taken with the 4 1/2-inch reflector showing the red spot and bands of Jupiter. This was the first time using this telescope the authors had seen the red spot and it was because of the enhancement techniques!

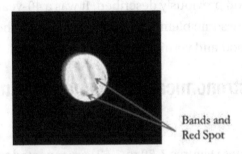

Bands and
Red Spot

Figure 7-52. *Enhanced Jupiter Image from 4 1/2-Inch Reflector, May 4, 2018*

The following Raspberry Pi code (Listing 7-3) was used to capture the videos that created single images which were then enhanced to create the preceding images. The faint numbers are line numbers for the code; they need to be deleted if the reader copies this code. Be sure that the indention for the program is identical to what is shown in the following. The indention is how the Python compiler knows what is in scope or not.

Listing 7-3. Raspberry Pi Code PI_SN004_Astrophotograhy_Video Capture

```
0   #Code Developed by Paul Bradt
1   import tkinter as tk
2   import picamera
3   import os
4   import traceback
5   import datetime
6   import time
7   import sys
8   import subprocess
9   from subprocess import Popen, PIPE, CalledProcessError
10  pwd = os.getcwd()
11  root = tk.Tk() #makes the window
12  root.geometry('200x1100+0+0')
13  camera = picamera.PiCamera()
14  root.wm_title("Camera GUI Program") #Makes the title that
    will appear in the top left
15  root.config(background = "#FFFFFF") #Sets background color
to  white
16  global now
17  #put widgets here
18  def picapture():
19      try:
```

```
20                      global now
21                      debugLog.insert(0.0, "Date Initialization Done\n")
22                      now = datetime.datetime.now().strftime("%F_%X")
23                      debugLog.insert(0.0, now + "\n")
24                      camera.start_preview (fullscreen=False,
                        window = (200,0,1100,640))
25                      camera.start_recording('/home/pi/' + now + '.h264')
26          except:
27                      print(traceback.format_exc(limit=10))
28  def stopcapture():
29                      camera.stop_recording()
30                      camera.stop_preview()
31  #Main Frame and its contents
32  mainFrame = tk.Frame(root, width=200, height = 900)
33  mainFrame.grid(row=0, column=1, padx=10, pady=2)
34  btnFrame = tk.Frame(mainFrame, width=200, height = 200)
35  btnFrame.grid(row=1, column=0, padx=10, pady=2)
26  debugLog = tk.Text(mainFrame, width = 20, height = 10,
    takefocus=0)
27  debugLog.grid(row=3, column=0, padx=10, pady=2)
28  cameraBtn = tk.Button(btnFrame, text="Start recording",
    command=picapture)
29  cameraBtn.grid(row=1, column=0, padx=10, pady=2)
30  stopBtn = tk.Button(btnFrame, text="Stop recording",
    command=stopcapture)
31  stopBtn.grid(row=2, column=0, padx=10, pady=2)
32  root.mainloop() #start monitoring and updating the
    GUI. Nothing  below here runs.
```

Image Creation and Enhancement from a Video

These excellent image enhancement techniques were provided by Jeff Dunehew. The first step is to convert the video to a useable format and then use it to create an improved image. There are three tools that the reader will need to download: VLC media player, PIPP, and Registax. Download the full version of Registax (size is about 3 MB).

> Converting the file to a normal video:
>
> To open the ".h264" files that the Raspberry Pi creates in Windows
>
> Install VLC player.
>
> Open VLC player.
>
> Drag the file onto the VLC player app.
>
> Note: You don't need to do this section; this is just to watch your video without doing any conversion.
>
> To prepare the file to convert:
>
> Open VLC player.
>
> Click Media ➤ Convert/Save.
>
> Click Add. Open the h264 file you saved that you want to convert.
>
> Then select the Convert/Save button at the bottom right.
>
> Select the destination toward the bottom of the next window. It will allow you to change file types if necessary. ".mp4" files seem to work great.

Once the file is converted to ".mp4", you want to use PIPP to align the video where the planet is always in the middle:

Open PIPP.

Drag the ".mp4" video into the file window.

Check the planetary radio button at the bottom of the window.

Click Processing on the menu at the top and then start processing.

Once it is done, it will create a PIPP file folder in whatever directory your original ".mp4" video was in. The new video in the PIPP folder will have the planet aligned in the middle and will have an .avi format.

Registax is the tool that will rip the images out of the video and stack them in order to enhance the image. The following steps are what the authors used to create some of the images in this book.

There are several steps that the astronomer needs to take when using Registax. It is also a bit of trial and error to obtain images that are enhanced without too much enhancement:

1. Load the .avi file that was created using PIPP into Registax.

2. To set the alignment points, it is best to step through the frames of the video and find a good image that has the features you want to use for alignment. Click each alignment point. Registax leaves a little circle for each alignment point.

3. To do the alignment, click Align, and then the software goes through the video and tries to find key images that have the alignment points and then lines them up.

4. This step is a bit of trial and error; this process is called limit, and it tells Registax how to limit the number of frames used for the stacking process. The astronomer needs to select either the best percentage of frames to use or the actual number of best frames to use. Again this requires a bit of trial and error.

Then click Limit to reduce it down to the frames selected.

5. Next, click Stack. Stacking images creates a single image with the focused parts of all the images.

6. After it is finished stacking the images, click the Wavelet tab and use the slider bars to adjust the image to enhance it.

7. Once the astronomer has a clean enhanced image they are happy with, they need to save it.

The following YouTube video is a very good overview of this process:

www.youtube.com/watch?v=JkTiVdx3OCQ

Recap of Example Images and Enhancement Techniques

This section shows a few images captured by the authors and provides a high-level overview of some of the tools and techniques used to enhance and create some spectacular images of the two largest planets in the Solar System.

Summary

This chapter provides the reader with some very exciting projects that expand on the use of the Arduino and Raspberry Pi to capture and record data regarding light and astronomical images in a way that would have been impossible just a few short years ago. The introduction of powerful devices like the light sensor and advanced digital cameras makes this possible. Add on the ability to utilize and share the data via computers, and again that approaches the original *Star Trek* tricorder!

APPENDIX

Reference Material

This appendix contains some additional useful information regarding various projects in this book.

Soldering Safety

Soldering can be an enjoyable experience, but occasionally a difficult soldered connection can also be a frustrating experience. These tips will help to make it a safe experience. First, make sure you understand the basics of soldering. If unsure, take a basic class in electronics:

- Practice on scrap wires.

- Use fixtures or objects to hold the pieces in the proper configuration.

- Avoid breathing the fumes from the soldering iron.

- Always remember the soldering iron tip and recently heated soldered connections are very hot.

- Always remember to wear safety glasses to protect your eyes.

- Remove flammable objects from the area.

© Paul Bradt and David Bradt 2020
P. Bradt and D. Bradt, *Science and Engineering Projects Using the Arduino and Raspberry Pi*,
https://doi.org/10.1007/978-1-4842-5811-8

General Shop Safety

This section contains some good shop practices to keep the reader safe:

- Always, always use eye protection; it is amazing the number of times something will come loose when working on it.

- Use extreme care when handling sharp objects like saws, knives, or screwdrivers. Again, when using these items, you can slip or lose control and accidentally cut yourself.

- Use caution and be very careful when using power tools. They are made to cut or remove metal or wood material. The reader's hand is much softer material and will be easily cut or bruised.

- Finally, it is a very good idea to stop before doing a job and think about what could go wrong. Ask questions like "Is that frayed electrical cord going to short out?" or "Is that box balanced on top of things going to fall when I work under it?" This is the start of good job hazard analysis and is very important to work safely.

Manufacturing Techniques

The force sensor used in the zero gravity and friction experiments needs to have wires soldered to be able to connect it to the Arduino. Figure A-1 shows how the sensor and wires were held in place to do the soldering using a piece of scrap wood and some tape.

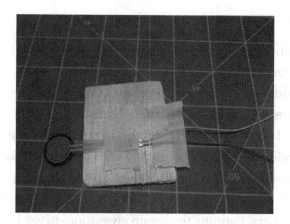

Figure A-1. *Soldering Technique for Force Sensor*

Soldering

Tips (if the researcher is unfamiliar with soldering, please read section "Soldering Safety" first):

1. Start on one wire.

    A. Strip the wires.

    B. It is easier with these connections to bend up one lead at a time.

    C. Solder the wires by touching the solder iron tip to the connection and then adding a little solder.

    D. Move the shrink tubing up the sensor to cover the solder joint. Make sure it goes up to the sensor.

    E. Use a heat gun to melt the shrink tubing. The soldering iron can be used, but be very careful to only touch it very lightly, and move it quickly away from the tip.

2. Repeat on the other wire.

Another slightly tricky soldering job is the wire harness to the MCP9700 sensor used in the rod conduction project and the convection project. Figure A-2 shows the assembled sensor. The authors found the best way to solder this is to bend one leg up, slide the heat shrink tubing onto the wire, make the solder connection, slide the heat shrink tubing down, and shrink it. Finally, bend it back in line with the others. Bending the leg up gives room to work. Be careful to not break the wire. Do the other two connections the same way. Make sure not to break the leg off the transitor.

Figure A-2. *MCP9700 Temperature Sensor and Wire Harness*

Basic Arduino and Raspberry Pi Python Commands

The following list is a handy starting point to understand some common Arduino and Raspberry Pi Python commands. It is meant to help someone very new to these devices get a basic understanding of these commands.

Some Key Arduino Code Commands

The following code commands are used extensively in most Arduino programs. This list is a good place to start when learning how to program an Arduino:

- Int: Defines a variable as an integer.

- #include: Used to designate additional libraries to be used by code.

- Serial.begin: Starts up serial communication and sets the data rate. Typically, we use it at rate 9600 baud.

- Float: Sets up floating point values for numbers used in the code.

- AnalogRead: Reads values from the selected analog port.

- Print: Prints data to the serial port.

- Println: Prints a blank line to the serial port in addition to what is in ("").

- Delay: This command halts the Arduino from doing anything for the allotted time in msec.

- Return: This is used to return to the caller with a value. For example, X = Math.add(2+3) will yield X = 5.

- Void: This sets up a function to not pass a value back to the caller, for example, public void functions(). X = functions() will throw an error in the compiler to remind the programmer to not expect a value.

Some Key Raspberry Pi Code Commands

The following code commands are used extensively in most Raspberry Pi programs. This list is a good place to start when learning how to develop Raspberry Pi programs:

- Import: Pull a third-party library which has its own set of code or function.

- def: Declare a function name and parameters.

- while: Do something while conditions are still true.

- print: Print to terminal a series of characters commonly referenced as string as an integer.

There are a lot of resources online that can help the reader gain an understanding of these and other commands. The Arduino site and the Raspberry Pi site are good places to get more information on commands and the format required so that they work.

3D Printing

This is a very new and exciting technology. There is a bit of a learning curve; however, there are a lot of helpful resources available including online help and maker spaces, and some libraries now have 3D printers too.

The authors first used the 3D printers at a local library to get experience and then purchased a small 3D printer as the price came down (Figure A-3). This technique has brought the concept of the *Star Trek* replicator to life.

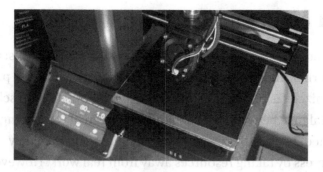

Figure A-3. *Low-Cost 3D Printer*

Computer-Aided Design Options

3D printing requires a special type of file format. Typically it is an ".stl" file format. The authors have not tried all of the following tools listed but have heard that they can be used to create the files needed for 3D printing.

Often, each CAD system operates a little differently, so the reader is encouraged to try out a few and determine which one they find easier to use:

- Blender
- FreeCAD
- Fusion 360
- Tinkercad
- SketchUp

Once the .stl file is created, then this file will need to be loaded into a slicer program. This tool takes the solid object and breaks it down into a form that the 3D printer can use to create each slice. A popular slicer program is CURA which supports many of the common 3D printers.

Project Management for Engineering

There are many different project management scheduling tools: Gantt charts, waterfall, and others. They are very useful to lay out the project in a nice organized fashion and helpful to ensure completion on schedule. There is a balance between the schedule and the real work being accomplished. For small projects, a very detailed schedule may actually hinder progress by taking resources away from real work. However, on a big project, a detailed Gantt chart (Figure A-4) may actually ensure success by capturing all of the critical tasks needed. These tools are very useful for engineering projects.

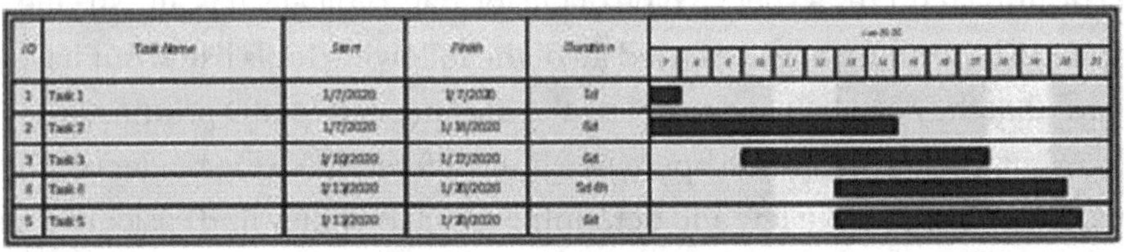

Figure A-4. *Example Gantt Schedule*

Decision Analysis for Engineering

Comparing options and determining the correct choice to make is a key aspect of decision analysis. One technique is to evaluate various factors and determine a comparative measure on these key factors. Pugh analysis is one example of this technique (Table A-1).

Table A-1. *Example Pugh Option Analysis*

Factors	Base Case	Option 1	Option 2	Option 3
Price	Datum	Plus	Minus	Minus
Reliability	Datum	Minus	Minus	Plus
Annual cost	Datum	Equal	Plus	Equal
Ease of use	Datum	Minus	Plus	Equal
Options	Datum	Equal	Equal	Plus
Score	0	-1	0	1

Thermal Conductivity Coefficients

The following are some thermal conductivity coefficients for various materials. Data is from source [1]:

- Copper thermal conductivity coefficients
  h = 380 Joule/sec-m-°C

- Aluminum thermal conductivity coefficients
  h = 200 Joule/sec-m-°C

- Steel thermal conductivity coefficients
  h = 40 Joule/sec-m-°C

- Glass thermal conductivity coefficients
  h = 0.84 Joule/sec-m-°C

- Brick thermal conductivity coefficients
  h = 0.84 Joule/sec-m-°C

- Wood thermal conductivity coefficients
  h = 0.1 Joule/sec-m-°C

Coefficients of Friction

The following are some frictional coefficients for various materials. Data is from source [1]:

Wood on wood

μs = 0.4

μk = 0.2

Metal on metal (lubricated)

μs = 0.15

μk = 0.07

Steel on steel (unlubricated)

μs = 0.7

μk = 0.6

Rubber on dry concrete

μs = 1.0

μk = 0.8

Astronomy Terms

- Alti-azimuth: Two-axis telescope mount that when controlled moves vertically and rotates to the position. It tracks the apparent star motion due to the Earth's rotation by moving in both vertical and horizontal rotating directions.

- Aperture: A hole or opening that light passes through, which aids in controlling the amount of light entering a camera or telescope.

- Equatorial telescope mount: This is a fairly simple telescope mount that has one axis pointing at the North Star and then needs only to rotate around that axis to compensate for the Earth's rotation.

- Focal length: Measure of a telescope that when combined with the lens provides a measure of the magnification. Physically, it is the distance between a lens or curved mirror and its focal point.

- Terminator: The line between night and day on the moon or Earth.

- Telescope yoke: The structure on a telescope, commonly "U" shaped, that supports the telescope and other equipment, usually enabling telescope adjustments in the vertical axis.

Specifications of the Meade ETX-60AT

The Meade ETX-60AT (Figure A-5) is a nice little telescope that does not require much storage space and can be set up quickly. It has the Autostar computer controller that allows it to track the stars as the Earth rotates. For its size, this telescope does an amazing magnification job. It shows a lot of detail on several solar system planets and the moon.

Figure A-5. *Meade ETX-60AT*

It is no longer available directly from Meade, but ETX-60AT and
ETX-70AT scopes are on sale on eBay, ranging in price from $65 to $100.
The clamping mechanism and shelf described in Chapter 7 should work
with either the ETX-60AT or ETX-70AT. By adding the Raspberry Pi 3 ($185)
and its hardware to one of these telescopes, the astronomer has an updated,
modern telescope with minicomputer, touchscreen, and camera for $270.
A new equivalent telescope without a camera costs about $300–350.

Meade ETX-60AT telescope specifications:

- Aperture: 60mm

- Focal length: 350mm

- Maximum practical visual power: 200×

- Optical tube dimensions: 3.6" × 14.6"

- Overall dimensions: 15.9″ × 7″ × 9″

- Telescope and Autostar weight: 6.7 lbs (8 lbs with Pi)

- Alti-azimuth drive system using servo motors and encoders

- Battery life for Autostar: ≈ 20 hrs

Setup, Updates, and Repairs

The Autostar control (Figure A-6) system requires a little time for the novice astronomer to develop utilization proficiency, but once she/he becomes familiar with it, it works well.

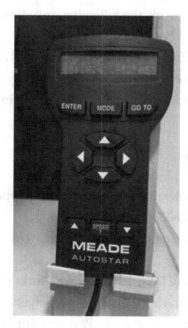

Figure A-6. *Autostar Controller*

After stepping through the initial screen and time setup, do a telescope alignment. The first step is to align the telescope so it is horizontal and pointing at the North Star. The Autostar will prompt the astronomer through the next steps, but basically it will move to a bright stellar object. The astronomer indicates it is good. Then it will move to a second bright stellar object. After the astronomer indicates it is good again, it will tell you it is ready to find another object and it is ready to use.

The software in the Autostar contains a catalog of stellar objects and can be updated so that orbits and information are current.

See the Meade web site for instructions and what is required to do this update: `www.meade.com/support/auto.html`.

Additionally, if you purchase a used telescope, verify that all the motors and adjustment functions are working. If the drives on your Meade telescope do not work, the following web site can help with repairs: `www.youtube.com/watch?v=qbNwBWB29ow`.

You can also find other videos by searching YouTube. They show how to repair the drives that move the telescope vertically in each yoke and how to repair the drive that rotates the telescope around in the base.

Helpful Books

D. Giancoli, Physics for Scientists and Engineers, Upper Saddle River: Pearson Prentice Hall, 2008.

E. Premeaux and B. Evans, Arduino Projects to Save the World, New York: Apress, 2011.

F. Kreith, Principles of Heat Transfer, New York: Harper & Row, 1973.

M. Banzai, Getting Started with Arduino, Sebastopol: O'Reilly, 2011.

M. L. James, G. M. Smith, and J. C. Wolford, Applied Numerical Methods for Digital Computation, New York: Harper & Row, 1977.

S. Monk, Programming Arduino Next Steps, New York: McGraw Hill, 2014.

Index

© Paul Bradt and David Bradt 2020
P. Bradt and D. Bradt, *Science and Engineering Projects Using the Arduino and Raspberry Pi*,
https://doi.org/10.1007/978-1-4842-5811-8

C

D

E

Printed in the United States
By Bookmasters